MAN

in

GOD'S MILIEU

by

BASTIAN KRUITHOF

BAKER BOOK HOUSE ● GRAND RAPIDS, MICHIGAN

Library of Congress Catalog Card Number: 68-19211

PHOTOLITHOPRINTED BY CUSHING - MALLOY, INC.
ANN ARBOR, MICHIGAN, UNITED STATES OF AMERICA
1 9 6 8

2348

TO THE MEMORY

OF

PETER G. BERKHOUT, M.D., M.Sc.

WHO

STUDIED THE FULL REVELATION

AND

EXPERIENCES IT NOW

Preface

Throughout the years several of my friends, knowing my interests, have urged me to write a book on Christianity and culture. Gathering the pollen from hundreds of sources has been a fascinating experience. Making the finished product a matter of simple communication has been difficult, but inspiration has won over perspiration.

This book is an attempt to approach an enduring problem from a Biblical, theological, and philosophical point of view. I am grateful to all those from whom I have learned, whether as teachers in classrooms or writers of a literature more vast than I can acknowledge. My shortcomings are not laid to their charge.

I am also grateful to Hope College for granting me the Julia Reimold Faculty Award, which made possible the writing of this book; to the Baker Book House, whose publishing efforts are doing so much to keep Christian scholarship alive; and to my patient wife, who, giving me encouragement, has weathered the incessant pounding of the typewriter and the many hours of silent companionship.

Contents

Man, the Thinking Reed

The stars look down, and as far as we know mortal man is the only creature who is aware of it. If he reflects a moment, he knows that the stars really do not look down; they are not aware of him and therefore are not concerned. In other words man differs from the universe in which he is a wanderer, a seeker, and a finder.

He is this because in greater or lesser degree he has the power to think. If he is honest enough, he will admit his limitations. If he is wise, he will listen to Pascal who reminds him that "man is a reed, but he is a reed that thinks."[1] And he will hear from this searching mind more concerning the grandeur and the misery of man.

How much one can read into Rodin's "The Thinker" very likely depends on the viewer. The original in Philadelphia, a replica facing the philosophy building on Columbia University's campus, or the book ends on my desk leave the field wide open. At least the sculptor sets one to thinking.

There are those today who speak with jubilation about man's coming of age. But with us are more than the echoes of the predicament of modern man and the sickness of Western civilization. For the discerning the roots of glory and of decay are there.

Long ago Protagoras said that "man is the measure of things," but for decades man has been taking the measure of himself and come up with fully as much gloom as glory. Omar Khayyam found no answers to the riddle of life. Bertrand

Russell speaks of "the slow, sure doom falling pitiless and dark"[2] on us all. Albert Camus in gloomy existentialist mood refers to "the benign indifference of the universe." Others like Heiddeger and Sartre present man battling it out in his own cellophane wrapper, whatever the *it* may be.

While scientists turn out their gemini capsules and aim at the moon with other than a lover's gaze, some writers of fiction and drama are more concerned with man in the sty than in the sky. In the portrayal of what man is there is the suggestion of what he ought to be, but when man is left to himself, there is little of redemption.

Is man only a two-legged beetle, a forked radish, an ant on a whirling planet, or is he something more? At least he must admit that he is related to the universe. Moreover, if he does any reflecting at all, he should ask himself if the universe is friendly or hostile. He should do this with more depth than the society woman who said to Carlyle, "I accept the universe." The dour Scot's reply should set us to thinking: "Gad, she'd better."

There are those who are sure that acceptance of our place in a cosmic environment solves little or nothing. Does life have its highest meaning within the framework of the universe, or do we perhaps need God? It is the Christian who assumes that we do.

Even though man does not think as much and as well as he ought, he does some reflecting. He also reacts to others and to his environment with more than his mind. He believes, he dreams, he loves, he responds as a person. Though he is part of the physical order, he does not consider himself an *it*. He is alive. He has physical characteristics that differentiate him from animals and the inanimate world. Because there are others besides himself, he is a social being. He has the gift of language. He makes distinctions between good and bad. He is more or less creative with his mind and his hands. He knows something about, and may even engage in worship.

Assured of all this man may still be a riddle to himself.

Living in an age resounding with knowledge explosion, he must admit, if he is honest, that he has a hunger for knowing more about himself.

Artists and thinkers have puzzled over this problem. Shakespeare's Hamlet gives us a picture of Renaissance man.

> What a piece of work is man! how noble in reason! how infinite in faculty! in form and moving how express and admirable! in action how like an angel! in apprehension how like a god! the beauty of the world! the paragon of animals![3]

But he adds: "Man delights not me."

Pascal's parody on these words opens more doors that lead to greater understanding.

> What a chimera, then, is man! what a novelty! what a monster, what a chaos, what a subject of contradiction, what a prodigy! A judge of all things, feeble worm of the earth, depositary of the truth, sewer of uncertainty and error, the glory and the shame of the universe.[4]

By indirection the point is that man in search of himself could do better by looking beyond himself. But even in attempting this man has stayed quite close to himself as center. A look at several views of man bears this out.

The Greek or classical view stresses reason. Reason seeks and finds the good. It must control the passions as Plato's myth of the charioteer in the *Phaedrus* illustrates. That makes for the proper control of soul, mind, and body. For Aristotle it is the rational man who acquires *eudaimonia,* or happiness.

It is true that knowledge about man requires thinking about him as subject and object. When Socrates turned his thoughts inward away from the universe where the pre-Socratics wandered and wondered, he did so on the advice of the Delphic oracle: "Know thyself." Living in a pre-Christian age, he busied himself with the search for the true, the good, and the beautiful. He sensed the transcendent, and his concern was with destiny and destination. His conversation as given in the *Crito* and the *Phaedo* dealt with the immortality of the soul.

Whereas the Greek inquirer and his disciple, Plato, were taken up with man in relation to the eternal, the typical Renaissance man, though perhaps paying lip-service to the essentials of the Christian faith, preferred one world at a time and more likely this one. He stressed the importance of the individual as a revolt against the authoritarianism of the Church. Man was able to take care of himself quite well in all fields.

The adventurous spirit spurred on the advancement of learning, brought on a florescence in the arts, produced a lasting literature, and discovered new continents. Man was in the saddle of winged horses, riding hard, pursuing the ideal of the complete man: health of body, strength of character, and wealth of mind.

We must not forget that during these times there were others whose thoughts went beyond man. Savonarola's fiery preaching in Florence brought him to the flames. Artists like Leonardo da Vinci and Michelangelo, creating composites of pagan and Christian thought, gave us *The Last Supper* and *The Last Judgment*.

It is well to keep in mind also that the northern humanists like Erasmus, More, and Colet were Christians who strove to keep the hemlock and the cross together, drinking from the springs of Helicon as well as from the Jordan.

The Age of Reason, culminating in the eighteenth century, is a long pilgrimage of the mind. It is marked by continued stirrings in the areas of the natural sciences and a rebirth of philosophy. Emphasis on man as thinker led to a frigid rationalism expressed even in the religious life, and to the scepticism of Hume who roused Immanuel Kant from his dogmatic slumbers. It was Kant who strove to prove that pure reason can deal only with the phenomenal, and that it requires the practical reason to deal with God, Freedom, and Immortality.

It is understandable that there were protests culminating in the Romantic movement with its soaring delight in the spirit of man, and the Wesleyan revival stressing man's need for God and salvation.

The nineteenth century brought its jarring note. Darwin's theories on evolution, popularized by Huxley, ruffled the surface of Victorian placidity. It is evident in Matthew Arnold's

>Wandering between two worlds, one dead,
>The other powerless to be born.[5]

and in Tennyson's fluctuations in "In Memoriam" and the "Locksley Hall" poems.

Moreover, higher criticism, especially in Germany, approached the Bible as literature, undermining foundations that had stood for centuries, and shocking the faith that held to the inerrancy of the Word.

The jolting has carried on into our century. There are those who are satisfied with a religious humanism or naturalism that is agnostic about the supernatural. God as an idea or symbol is created in man's image like Santa Claus or Uncle Sam. A variety of opinions about God and Jesus Christ empties the word *Christian* of specific meaning except perhaps in an ethical sense.

In the nineteenth century August Comte maintained that man has left the theological and philosophical stages behind and has entered the scientific. His descendants, the logical positivists, are immersed in linguistics. Man must be concerned about words that have meaning. If a word has no referrent, it is folly to use it. God and values are vague terms. You cannot touch them with your finger. They evaporate before logic.[6]

It is absurd to deny that words and meanings are very important. But what thinkers engaged in linguistics seem to forget is that man lives by more than logic and definitions. They do not explain how the whole man embraces his wife and children, is awed by a sunset and moved by music, and is challenged by the soul's invincible surmise.

For decades existentialism has been in the news to the extent that it may become a household word. Attempts to define it may prove futile. Perhaps it is best to consider it as a mood rather than a philosophy.

Existentialism owes much to Sören Kierkegaard, "the melancholy Dane in whom Hamlet was mastered by Christ," as Forsyth puts it.[7] In his lifetime he made an impact on his own country, but not beyond. It was in the first decades of our century, especially after the First World War, that his writings came to light. His caustic thoughts appealed to the disillusioned who saw no hope in dreams, and schemes, and systems.

The Dane had written: "It is the misfortune of our age that it has too much knowledge, that it has forgotten what it means to live." He had said that mankind was bogged down in "the mudbanks of reason." His criticism was aimed at the rationalism of Hegel, the pursuit of objectivity. He felt that "the system" had invaded theology and the Church. His appeal was to "that solitary individual." Like a Socratic gadfly he attacked massification, and maintained that "truth is subjectivity."[8]

By this he did not mean that the individual creates truth, but that he must experience it in the sense of involvement and decision. For Kierkegaard, man in his loneliness must make the leap of faith. It seems absurd, but it is the only way that fulfills his destiny. Even then he is not a Christian but is always becoming one. To exist means just that.

Man can pass through three stages. There is the aesthetic in which he, like Faust, Don Juan, and the Wandering Jew, seeks fulfillment but ends in frustration and despair. There follows the ethical stage in which he shows concern for the good and finds his proper relation to God and man.[9] Finally there is the religious stage in which by the leap of Faith he finds rest in God.

The incisive terminology of Kierkegaard has been woven into the texture of existentialism. Its effects are evident in philosophy, theology, literature, and drama. Terms like anxiety, despair, the absurd, involvement, decision, confrontation are used by thinkers miles apart as to identification.

Broadly speaking we can identify two types of existentialists. There is the atheistic kind that has dismissed the supernatural but stresses the importance and freedom of individual personality. A person has will and choice as well as reason. He is free to suffer courageously, though he does not know the outcome for certain. Striving valiantly, man is in an egocentric cell from which, according to Sartre, there is no exit.

According to Sartre it would change nothing whether God exists or not. The believer is in the same position as the unbeliever. For self is taken up with inwardness. Moved by a nostalgia for the past and anticipation for the future, man remains an exile.

In Greek mythology Sisyphus was condemned to roll a stone uphill endlessly. At each near-success the stone would roll down, and the doomed effort would begin again. Such courageous but hopeless striving epitomizes the gloomy existentialist.

There is another kind of existentialism that is linked with the Christian faith. It is more in the spirit of Kierkegaard. Gabriel Marcel is one of its leading representatives. Christian thinkers of this type maintain that the subjective experience of man is in touch, not with Nothing, but with a Being. God confronts man with His grace, with the affirmation of the Word made flesh. Reason may be scandalized by the absurdity, but faith as the response of the whole man reaches out to God who has reached out to man.

The dilemma or predicament of man is there for those who are concerned and for those who are not. There is concern on the part of those who, like Camus, believe that this world has no ultimate meaning, but that there must be some meaning because man is here, and he is the only creature who insists on deciphering it. However, whatever value life has is centered in man. There is no supernatural revelation to enlighten him.

There is concern also on the part of those who hold that reason, though eloquent, cannot give the final answer. For them faith, and more particularly the Christian faith, is essential. These face the perennial and perplexing problem of reason and faith with the assurance that in the great adventure of the whole man faith in God is necessary to clearer understanding.

An airing of the relation between reason and faith may prove helpful. This we must do. And after that it is important to ponder the concept of revelation which casts light on both reason and faith. That way we become better acquainted with man and with the revealing God who makes Himself known in words and events that have changed the course of history and put content into the human pilgrimage.

NOTES

1. Blaise Pascal, *Pensées* (New York: Modern Library), p. 116.
2. Bertrand Russell, *Selected Papers* (New York: Modern Library), "A Free Man's Worship," pp. 15, 16.
3. Act II, Sc. 2.
4. Pascal, *op. cit.,* p. 143.
5. "Stanzas From the Grande Chartreuse"
6. The plight of contemporary philosophy is admirably treated in *Time*, January 7, 1966.
7. P. T. Forsyth, *The Work of Christ* (London: Independent Press, 1946), p. XXXII.
8. These thoughts are scattered throughout his journals and many of his books.
9. See especially Sören Kierkegaard's *Either-or* (Gloucester: Peter Smith), 2 vols.

II

Reason and Faith

The problem of reason and faith is a knotty one that has perplexed and stimulated man for ages. Stressing one aspect of the problem at the expense of the other will not solve the riddle of life. For man is potentially a thinking being whose reason discovers limitations, and whose faith yearns for wholeness. Like Sophocles he would like "to see life steadily and see it whole." Pitting reason against faith or faith against reason is not the way to understanding. Both are essential in the search for meaning.

Reason

Philosophy deals especially with reason. It is concerned with the *whence,* the *why*, and the *whither.* Man's life can be summed up in three words: discontent, quest, certainty. There are those who seem to be satisfied with the quest, but uncommon common sense reminds us that seeking is in order to finding or being found.

Man asks questions, hoping for answers. Therefore, as Warren C. Young says, "[He] must philosophize or fossilize."[1]

This may seem small comfort for those who hold that philosophy makes clear things muddy. But serious living, which implies a measure of reflection, should ponder these words of Hibben: "The problems of philosophy are . . . the problems of life, the burden of the mystery of existence, the origin and destiny of man, the relations which he sustains to the world of which he is a part, and to the unseen universe which lies round about him."[2]

The long history of philosophy should bring home to us the significance of these words: "One who has not lived in the Republic of Plato, searched with Aristotle or Hegel for the first principles of things, experienced the Copernican revolution with Kant, or lived with Spinoza *sub specie acternitatis* has missed looking at the world through some of the grandest windows which human reason has opened to illuminate man's primitive darkness."[3]

The study of man is always at the heart of philosophy but man in relation, for no human being is an island as Donne said. The pre-Socratics were concerned with the nature of ultimate reality. Socrates, heeding the advice of the Delphic oracle, chose the maxim: "Know thyself." His confessed ignorance was the prelude to wisdom. However, in him as in Plato, there is always the higher reference, man's relation to the eternal verities. The discourses on the immortality of the soul disclose the noblest reaches of pagan thought.[4]

Pagan thinking even with the higher reference gave the edge to reason. It held that knowledge is virtue, and consequently that ignorance is sin. It failed to emphasize the will which can be as bent and twisted as the reason. To know the true and the good does not insure the doing of these. Saint Paul had a better insight into human nature when he complained that he did not do the good he wanted but the evil he did not want. He considered himself a wretched man who needed deliverance (Romans 7).

This giving the edge to reason without admitting its limitations is a great part of the story of philosophy. Kant sensed the limitations. In his *Critique of Pure Reason* he concluded that reason can deal only with phenomena, not with noumena. He found it necessary to write his *Critique of Practical Reason,* in which he proposed the three postulates of God, Freedom, and Immortality. Though it was not a concession to the Christian faith, it was a plea for a rational religion.

Reason cannot escape the impact of faith. That is why there is also the philosophy of religion. It denies the importance of detached reason. It maintains that right reason is the whole man thinking. Reason may not exclude emotion, will, and experience. According to Nels Ferré, "Right religion [in which right reason plays an important part] is our fully positive whole-response to the complete combination of what is most important and real."[5]

Man's thinking cannot ignore religion which presupposes an ideal, spiritual reality above the mere empirical reality. Both religion and philosophy are concerned with the ultimate. Elton Trueblood suggests that belief in God may be true or false; it is never trivial. If the essence of philosophy is to think, the essence of religion is to dedicate.[6] William Temple puts it well when he says, "Philosophy seeks knowledge for the sake of understanding while religion seeks knowledge for the sake of worship." Again he writes, "The heart of religion is not an opinion about God . . ., it is a personal relation with God."[7]

Religion, therefore, requires thinking as well as believing. Plato said that the unexamined life is not worth living. So we can say that the unexamined faith is not worth having.

But reason, whether it deals with religion or not, should be marked by humility. Reason implies doubting, but it should distinguish between the right and the wrong kinds of doubt. Galileo was correct when he said, "Doubt is the father of discovery." And Browning's Rabbi ben Ezra made a point when he said:

> Rather I prize the doubt
> Low kinds exist without;
> Finished and finite clods,
> Untroubled by a spark.

It is also beneficial that reason should at times make us doubt our doubts. In order to take in whole truth it should become religious. For how can one reason about religion unless one is religious. At least one should respect such religious reason as is found in the experienced writers of the Bible, in such men as Augustine, Aquinas, Luther, Calvin, Pascal, Kierkegaard, Barth, Brunner, John Baillie, Herman Bavinck, Abraham Kuyper, T. S. Eliot, C. S. Lewis, and hundreds more.

Reason and faith speak to man's wholeness in the lives of these thinking believers. To them apply the touching words of William Temple's conclusion in his Gifford Lectures:

> Natural Theology (based largely on reason) ends in a hunger for that Divine Revelation which it began by excluding from its purview. Rightly sifting with relentless criticism every argument, it knows what manner of Voice that must be which shall promise relief to mankind; but the Voice is not its own, nor can it judge the message that is spoken. "Come unto me . . . and I will give you rest"; it is not philosophy that can estimate the right of the Speaker to issue that invitation or to make that promise; that right can be proved or disproved only by the experiment of life.[8]

Faith

The experiment of life involves believing as well as thinking. Even those who reason best or think they do have some kind of faith. It expresses itself in the acceptance of the dignity of man, democracy, the uniformity of nature, the significance of the scientific steps of mathematical processes, authorities, or the acceptance of oneself and one's fellowman.

Religious faith, however, reaches out and up and lays hold of the invisible which to devout souls is most real. This surmise is expressed well by Francis Thompson in "The Kingdom of God":

> O world invisible, we view thee,
> O world intangible, we touch thee,
> O world unknowable, we know thee,
> Inapprehensible, we clutch thee!

Faith from this point of view is not irrational. Augustine and others have insisted that we believe in order that we may understand. Faith and reason present us with a paradox, but both are essential. Pascal made much of the paradox. It is not a matter of "either - or," but of "both - and." A familiar statement of the Frenchman rings true: "The heart has its reasons, which reason does not know."[9] Faith has its right to its assumptions as well as reason has. It stresses the personal involvement and decision of the whole man who is always more than a logic chopper.

For Emil Brunner "faith is the reason which is opened to that which lies beyond reason."[10] Paul Tillich maintains that "faith is the state of being grasped by being itself."[11]

The Word of God cannot be understood without faith, more particularly the Christian faith. Hebrews 11 gives us a clear description of what faith in God really means. To prevent the possibility of losing oneself in abstractions, it goes on to show us what this faith meant to historical persons. The entire chapter presents a portrait gallery of the heroes and heroines of faith. They are concretely before us, real, genuine, and with something of the inferential which any painting implies.

These saints in the making and millions of others like them have experienced God, not as a blur, but as a reality. Though they acknowledge His transcendence, they also know Him as near. He is not an impassive Prime Mover, He is not lost in the vast spaces of the universe, nor is He limited by a three-story world of man's imagination, as Bishop Robinson presents it.

Pascal makes much of Isaiah's words: "Verily thou art a God who hidest thyself. . . ." That very fact, however, makes faith a challenge as well as a privilege and a responsibility. It also makes seeking, finding, and being found much more significant. Likewise it assures us that both faith and knowledge can be an adventure in which these grow from more to more.

Faith, therefore, has content. The Christian creeds, some of them written in blood, give expression to this. Of these the Apostles' Creed may be the best known, although it may not be thoroughly understood. Its nouns and verbs say much, but especially its verbs present the God of action who makes Himself known in events. Here revelation illumines certain facts in history. Jesus Christ is historical. In Him the supernatural impinges on the natural and gives meaning to it. Revelation enriches a reasonable faith, and both are essential to a meaningful commentary.

The creeds, doctrines, and standards of the Christian Church are not intended to freeze the content of faith, but to serve as synopses, guidelines, and maps that invite further exploration. If the Christian faith implies going back to the creeds and doctrines, and much better still, going back to the Scriptures on which these are based, it also implies a going forward with what is revealed. That way faith and knowledge take on the glorious adventure in the most exciting pilgrimage.

In contemporary terms faith as response to divine revelation is existential decision in regard to whole truth. The thrust is that faith is more than just intellectual assent, the accepting of a series of propositions. In theological writings today there seems to be an aversion to propositional truth. There is emphasis on involvement, decision, on the Word's grasping us at the moment. It is then that revelation has meaning for us. In a later chapter we shall have more to say about this emphasis, but for the present we admit that faith is more than intellectual assent and accepting of a series of propositions. In fact the Word of God and the creeds have said this long before certain of our contemporaries began hammering this home. The Christian faith at its best has always been a personal trust in a personal God who has made Himself known in the person of Jesus Christ and through the personal work of the Holy Spirit.

It is understandable that William Temple, John Baillie, Karl Barth, Emil Brunner, and others have stressed the importance of believing in God, for there is always the danger of accepting propositions without experiencing the faith. As Herman Bavinck put it long ago: "We must confess our faith, not simply believe our creeds." But the Word of God has said this long before and is saying it now.

There are those who are a bit critical of the Heidelberg Catechism's treatment of faith. In Lord's Day 7, Question 21 and its answer, we read of what true faith is.

> It is not only a certain knowledge by which I accept as true all that God has revealed to us in his Word, but also a wholehearted trust which the Holy Spirit creates in me through the Gospel, that, not only to others, but to me also God has given the forgiveness of sins, everlasting righteousness and salvation, out of sheer grace solely for the sake of Christ's saving work.

That "sure knowledge" which pertains to the truth that God has made known in his Word disturbs some. But this knowledge was never meant to be a mere acceptance of certain propositions. On the contrary it is an experiential knowledge of God Himself, We grasp it, not by means of some mystical experience, but by means of that unique revelation which culminates in Jesus Christ. He it is who gives concreteness to truth, for He Himself says: "I am the way, the truth, and the life." However, we would never have known Him nor what He said about Himself without the written Word.

The Catechism also speaks of "a wholehearted trust" and stresses salvation freely given by grace. This implies, not only decision, but also acceptance on our part.

Such faith in God includes trust, commitment, surrender, and faithfulness. It is also testimony to the faithfulness of God whose concern for the wayward is touchingly evident in His merciful approach. His entreating voice sounds clearly in such passages as the following: " 'Come now, let us reason together, says the Lord . . .' " (Isaiah 1:18); " 'Ho, every one who thirsts, come to the waters' " (Isaiah 55:1); " 'Come to me, all who labor and are heavy-laden, and I will give you rest' " (Matthew 11:28).

Another important factor in the Christian faith is its application. After his most doctrinal statements Paul always turns to the moral life and does so in detail. For what is faith without concern for the good life? And James tells us that faith without works is dead. The ethical teachings of the Old Testament prophets and of Jesus, as for example in the Sermon on the Mount, undergird the strong Scriptural directive that morals are to faith as fruit is to trees. This emphasis is strongly made in the third part of the Catechism which develops the meaning of gratitude expressed in good works. The critics would do well to read it again. Awaiting them and us all is the discovery that the Christian faith is the dynamic of action.

The Christian maintains, therefore, that faith and reason are complementary. Stressing one at the expense of the other leads to extremes, either a cold rationalism or an absurd fanaticism. It is more than "the Wager" of Pascal as he himself would admit. It is more than "the leap" of Kierkegaard, which he also would admit. Faith is the higher reason which responds to who God is and to what He says about Himself and about man.

NOTES

1. Warren C. Young, *A Christian Approach to Philosophy* (Wheaton: Van Kampen Press, 1954), p. 20.
2. John G. Hibben, *The Problems of Philosophy* (New York: Scribners, 1898).
3. R. F. Piper and P. W. Ward, *The Fields and Methods of Knowledge* (New York: Crofts, 1929), p. 370.
4. See especially the *Crito* and *Phaedo.*
5. Nels Ferré, *Faith and Reason* (New York: Harper, 1946), p. 4.
6. Elton Trueblood, *Philosophy of Religion* (New York: Harper, 1957), p. 8.
7. William Temple, *Nature, Man, and God* (London: Macmillan, 1951), pp. 30 and 54.
8. *Ibid.,* p. 520.
9. Blaise Pascal, *Pensées* (New York: Modern Library), p. 95.
10. H. Emil Brunner, *Man in Revolt* (London: Lutterworth Press, 1939), p. 247.
11. Paul Tillich, *The Courage to Be* (Yale University Press, 1959), p. 156.

III

Revelation

In order to come to grips with Christianity and the problem of faith and reason one must understand what is meant by revelation. To anyone who does any reflecting at all the word implies a revealing, an enlightening on matters wholly or partly obscure. In matters of religion illumination is essential. As the eye thrives on light so the mind and heart of man respond to what is out there. In that manner what is outside becomes an inner experience. The disclosures of nature, the thoughts of men, the beauty of the arts, the march of history, the advances of science, all are givens about which man can think and write his commentary.

In contemporary theological thinking the concept of revelation has been subjected to searching analysis. Grateful for the renewed interest, we must also be critical of some conclusions. Today we hear much of God's self-disclosure, of His mighty acts, of confrontation, involvement, and the existential moment. All these are terms reminding us of the importance of a re-evaluation of what can easily become molded and moldy.

First of all in our study there is something to be said for an older understanding which speaks of two kinds of revelation: general and special. These deserve presentation and a careful evaluation.

General Revelation

By general revelation is meant God's disclosure in nature, history, and in the mind, heart, and conscience of man.

Scripture recognizes this revelation though it gives no comfort to those who would base their knowledge of God on unaided reason.

In Psalm 19 we read: "The heavens are telling the glory of God; and the firmament proclaims his handiwork." In Romans 1:18-20, Paul relates both the divine wrath and revelation to man's plight. He says, ". . . For what can be known about God is plain to them, because God has shown it to them. Ever since the creation of the world his invisible nature, namely, his eternal power and deity, has been clearly perceived in the things that have been made. So they are without excuse."

The implication is that man, because he is God's creature, still retains something of the sense of a divine presence no matter how low he has fallen. By virtue of creation he is basically religious.

The apostle goes on to show how man has degenerated religiously and morally. He has fashioned other gods who are not gods. His right relation to God severed, he has allowed himself to wallow in the mire of his basest passions.

If one is inclined to judge Paul as far too gloomy in his portrayal, he need only read the Roman historians and satirists who substantiate the apostle's indictment. Moreover the dark and seamy side of man is evident through long centuries up to the present day. One need not be a pessimist, as Paul certainly was not, to see the wretchedness of man torn loose from his original moorings.

That Paul does not despair is evident from his speeches at Lystra and in Athens, recorded in Acts 14 and 17. There also he uses the argument from general revelation, speaking of the God who has not left Himself without witness, and whose providence has extended to all mankind. He even quotes the pagan poets:

In him we live, and move and have our being.
For we are indeed his offspring.

General revelation, however, is not enough. Moreover a natural theology based on it is inadequate. The rationalism and deism of the eighteenth century, the Age of Reason, give more than a hint of what happens to God and to man when reason dominates faith. A natural theology based on general revelation does not satisfy the deepest longings of the heart, does not elicit the response of the whole man. As we have mentioned in Chapter II, William Temple puts the case touchingly in the concluding paragraphs of his Gifford Lectures.

The significance and the limitations of general revelation become apparent from another revelation which man needs, that is, the self-disclosure of God in the Scriptures and especially in Jesus Christ, the Word made flesh. Calvin speaks of this revelation as the spectacles through which we can appreciate the general. Moreover, the self-disclosure of God in His Word reveals more about God than the universe and the unaided mind of man can ever tell.

Special Revelation

General revelation illumined by the Word of God can tell us something about God. From this point of view creation discloses more than a hint of the divine majesty and greatness, an over-all providence, a goodness and a righteousness that make life worthwhile. But much more is needed. Therefore God has given us a revelation of His grace and love which answers to man's tragic light, a plight from which all his thinking and acting cannot release him. This revelation comes to us in words and events dealing with all that lies between the dawn of creation and the end of time, and always within the framework of the eternal.

Holy Scripture is the record of that revelation. According to Herman Bavinck "Scripture is not a human, accidental, arbitrary, defective addition to revelation, but it is itself an element in revelation. It is the enclosure and completion; it is the corner — and keystone of revelation."[1] Again he says, "The drive of the Holy Spirit was given to prophets and apostles and consisted in an awakening and a spurring on in order to make known the revelation of God's counsel which they had received."[2]

The Bible presents us with what Suzanne de Dietrich calls in the title of her book *God's Unfolding Purpose*. There is no philosophical approach, no speculation about God. His existence is taken for granted. God creates the universe and man. Man rebels and falls; and God steps in to lift man beyond tragedy. In Abraham He calls a special people who are to be the bearers of revelation. In their seed all the nations of the earth shall be blessed, and from their seed will come the Christ, the true Hope of Israel and of the world. In the fulness of time the Messiah comes to teach, to heal, to suffer, to die, and to rise again. Those who believe in Him, accepting His grace, become the Christian Church. The first chapter of the history of that Church is recorded in the Acts of the Apostles. And the continuing acts of God are evidenced in the zealous preaching and teaching, and in the healing, which together spread the Good News far and wide. Christ's orders, the Great Commission, bring about the expansion of Christianity. Kenneth Scott Latourette's massive volumes tell the story well.[3]

The Word of God reveals also the *telos,* the destiny and the destination of God's cause. Life, like an unfinished symphony, always has its inferential, but the indefiniteness is perhaps more baffling than consoling. The eschatology of revelation tells of a final consummation, of a Last Judgment, and the divine triumph expressed in the new heavens and the new earth in which the redeemed will dwell. Prophetic and apocalyptic language speaks of it poetically where prose falters. The idealism brings out the reality that is in preparation now.

Browning's "On earth the broken arc; in heaven the perfect round" may well be applied to the full story God is telling. Without the divine self-disclosure culminating in Jesus Christ and illumined by the Holy Spirit, man is the poorer. With this revelation man can grasp the meaning of existence. As Young says, "Special revelation must also be included among the criteria of truth, for it is the means relied upon to obtain truth of a specific kind in the Christian realistic world-view."[4]

We agree with G. C. Berkouwer that if we rule out the Word, we construct a revelation-concept which is simply a projection of our own subjectivity.[5] Moreover, the Word requires the illumination of the Holy Spirit in order to grasp what God is revealing.

The Prologue of John's gospel has great significance. The writer is not indulging in a Logos-speculation. For reason, Logos is an abstraction. For John, for the Christian believer, Christ is the personification, the incarnation of the Word. He is the eternal One, He was at the creation, He came into this world, and we beheld His glory. He said, "I am the way, the truth, and the life." It was because God so loved the world that He sent his only Son. Scripture does not reason from the cosmological to the soteriological, but rather the other way around. It is the redemptive revelation of God that explains the cosmological. Calvin sums it up well saying, "But faith is not conceived by the bare beholding of heaven and earth, but by the hearing of the Word."[6]

Current Views on Revelation

It is this very hearing of the Word of God that is in dispute today. Is the Bible the Word of God, or is the Word contained in the Bible as the older liberalism held? Is Biblical revelation propositional in character, or is the Word real only in the sense of personal encounter by which Truth becomes mine?

The existentialist mood has become the property and the romping ground of not a few theologians today. It expresses itself in a re-evaluation of the concept of revelation.

The emphasis is especially on truth as encounter and involvement. As a corollary the assertion is made that Biblical revelation is not propositional. The influence of Schleiermacher is there, and also that of Kierkegaard. It was the latter who, fighting against the dogmatism of "the system" and complaining that we are "stuck in the mud-bank of reason," insisted that "Truth is subjectivity."

By this statement he did not imply that man creates truth, but that when we are grasped by divine Truth in the moment, we have revelation. Faith is not a rational assent or a sub-scribing to authoritarian dogmatism, but a continual, fresh en-counter with the personal and historical event of God in Christ.

It was William Temple who rejected the conception of Scripture as a series of propositional truths. According to him God does not ask us to believe in a series of propositions but in Himself." What is offered to man's apprehension in any specific Revelation is not truth concerning God but the living God Himself."[7]

John Baillie echoes this thought also. "God does not give us information by communication; He gives us Himself in com-munion."[8]

Neo-orthodoxy, which must be credited with having given more than a jolt to the older liberalism, has many voices. Theologians like Barth, Brunner, Tillich, the Niebuhrs, Bon-hoeffer, and far to the left, Bultmann have their agreements and disagreements. But they do seem to have in common this view, that Scripture has more of the event-character than the proposition-character, and that revelation is the encounter be-tween Person and person.

Those who defend the propositional significance of Scripture do not deny the importance of the divine events, the Mighty Acts of God, and the one great divine Event in Jesus Christ which has a once-for-allness. They do not deny the reality of what happens when God by means of His revelation comes to grips with a person. Then surely the Word comes alive mean-ingfully in a personal experience such as is evident in the prophets and psalmists, the apostles after the Resurrection, Saul on the road to Damascus, and Lydia, and the Philippian jailor.

But how would we know this without the word-character of the Word? And how can we trust the account of these personal encounters if we are at liberty to trust or mistrust the written revelation? Moreover, if in places we mistrust the written Word, does it not imply a trusting in our own reason? That way lies the old rationalism which has never been kind to faith.

The Scriptures tell us a great deal about God, not only about what He has done and is doing, but also about who He is. "I AM WHO I AM." "I am the Lord, thy God." "Hear, O Israel, the Lord our God is one Lord." Such statements refer to being more than to doing, although they are spoken in the context of events. They do not exclude the Mighty Acts; but the acts have significance because of the Being who performs them.

So Jesus expressed Himself in those startling "I am" passages. There is no doubt about the acts He performed, but neither should there be doubts about who He is. Moreover, how could we know this about God and about His Son unless it were communicated? If we can mistrust some of the communication, what part of it can we trust? Can we even rely on the divine events or on some of them?

To be sure, the answer that truth becomes mine through encounter denies mere rationalism. But can it not also imply a sort of mysticism in which our personal faith takes on the aspect of a private revelation? Millions of persons may have this revelation, but what is there to solidify the experiences if there is no objective revelation that serves as a standard to justify the validity of the experiences? Is it not the Word and the Spirit, working together, that give us the assurance?

It is also necessary to consider what the Word says about itself. At this point it is wise to recall what Pascal advises: "He who will give the meaning of Scripture, and does not take it from Scripture, is an enemy of Scripture."[9]

Our Lord had great respect for the Old Testament and quoted from it often. He came, not to abolish the law and the prophets, but to fulfill them (Matthew 5:17). Every one who hears His words and does them is like the man building on the rock. Every one who hears His words but does not do them is like the man building on the sand (Matthew 7:24-27). Those who reject Him and do not receive His words have a judge; and His word will be their judge on the last day (John 12: 48).

Timothy is urged to merit God's approval as one who knows how to handle the Word of truth rightly (II Timothy 2:15). In the same letter we read that "All scripture is inspired by God and profitable for teaching, for reproof, for correction, and for training in righteousness" (3:16). In Ephesians 6:17 Paul refers to the sword of the Spirit which is the Word of God. Any good concordance will multiply proofs for propositional revelation which, illumined and applied by the Spirit, will enrich the Christian experience.

It all depends on what one's view of Scripture is. The evangelical maintains that the Word of God is inspired, and that its application to heart and mind and to hearts and minds in communion is the work of the Holy Spirit. Of course the Word presupposes personal encounter, but whether the encounter is there or not, it is still the revelation. It is the infallible rule of faith and life.

In recent years the Word as the revealed content of the Christian faith has been attacked by Bishop John A. T. Robinson of the Anglican Church. His sensational book, *Honest To God,* which Barth has called "an insipid booklet," is a digest (perhaps not fully digested) of Tillich, Bultmann, and Bonhoeffer. The aim is to present God and His revelation to contemporary man who is supposed to have come of age.

Veneration for the Word as divinely inspired and as written revelation has given way to a critical approach and a new idiom. The Bible records the experiences of men grasped by God. Modern man must attempt to get at the reality behind these experiences, and that requires an amount of demythologizing. Virgin Birth, Incarnation, and Resurrection are symbols rather than historical facts. Institutionalized Christianity, which has kept faith bottled up in the churches, must experience a breakthrough of dynamic faith expressing itself in "holy world-liness," in unconditional love for one's neighbor. What we need is a "religionless Christianity."

It would be foolish to deny the importance of a renewed emphasis on faith in action out there in the world. That is an old Biblical truth always new. Moreover, the impact of the Christian faith on the world throughout the centuries must not be minimized. The greater impact that should be made must also be stressed over and over again.

However, it remains problematical whether the man in the street who is supposed to have come of age will be able to un-derstand the new terminology. Or will it be "a tale told by an [idiom] full of sound and fury signifying [what]"? If man's place in the pew remains empty, and the Bible in his home gathers dust, what will the new approach convey to him? Will he experience "Thus saith the Lord" or "Thus spake Zarathus-tra," or "So says Bishop So-and So"? Or will his "religion" become entrenched more and more in subjectivism, vague, idealistic mysticism with perhaps a dash of pantheism?

The current approach to the Word goes hand in hand with the new morality. The Bible is no longer to be looked upon as absolute in its moral teachings. The Ten Commandments have had their day, and Jesus' concern is not to be taken seriously even though He came, not to abolish, but to fulfill the divine Law.

A more extensive treatment of the old and the new morality is reserved for Chapter XII.

In answer to those who proclaim the new idiom let it be said that evangelical Christianity at its best does not stand for dogmatic absolutism, frigid scholasticism, and faith without works of love. If it had succumbed to these, the Word would never have been "the shot heard round the world." But neither has it watered down the absoluteness of divine revelation as it comes to us in the Word, in Christ, and by the Spirit. Honoring the objective revelation that becomes meaningful in God's encounter with man, it refuses to succumb to an idiom that places reason above faith and transforms faith almost exclusively into morality.

In Isaiah 55:11 we read: ". . . so shall my word be that goes forth from my mouth; it shall not return to me empty, but it shall accomplish that which I purpose, and prosper in the thing for which I sent it."

We do well to ponder this from Him whose thoughts and ways are higher than our ways, yet not so high that He has left us without the witness. Emile Cailliet met God for the first time when he was given a Bible. He calls it "The Book That Understands Me."[10]

T. S. Eliot speaks to our time prophetically when he says:

> Where My Word is unspoken,
> In the land of lobelias and tennis flannels
> The rabbit shall burrow and the thorn revisit,
> The nettle shall flourish on the gravel court,
> And the wind shall say: "Here were decent godless
>   people:
> Their only monument the asphalt road
> And a thousand lost golf balls."

NOTES

1. Herman Bavinck, *Handleiding* (Kampen: J. H. Kok, 1913), p. 26.
2. Herman Bavinck, *Gereformeerde Dogmatiek* (Kampen: J. H. Kok, 1906), I, p. 38.
3. Kenneth Scott Latourette, *A History of the Expansion of Christianity,* (New York: Harper, 1937-1945), 7 vols.
4. Warren C. Young, *A Christian Approach to Philosophy* (Wheaton: Van Kampen Press, 1954), p. 57.
5. Gerrit C. Berkouwer, *General Revelation* (Grand Rapids: Eerdmans, 1955).
6. John Calvin, *New Testament Commentaries* (Grand Rapids: Eerdmans, 1960-1964), Commentary on Acts 14:17.
7. William Temple, *Nature, Man, and God* (London: Macmillan, 1951), p. 322.

8. John Baillie, *The Idea of Revelation* (New York: Columbia University Press, 1956), p. 47.

9. Blaise Pascal, *Pensées* (New York: Modern Library), p. 314.

10. *Christianity Today*, November 22, 1963. See also two excellent rebuttals by J. I. Packer, *Fundamentalism and The Word of God* (Grand Rapids: Eerdmans, 1962), and *Keep Yourselves From Idols* (Grand Rapids: Eerdmans, 1964).

IV

Theism

It is a fact not readily recognized by everyone that the Bible nowhere argues about the existence of God. It simply assumes Him. However, the writers use reason, language, and symbolic images to express their faith in Him.

Using our reason as well as our faith we find that the position suiting us best, answering to our deepest needs, is the theistic one. Theism implies a belief in one God who is not an *It* but a *Thou*. With this God we associate a purposive mind that gives an ultimate explanation of life and the universe. As personal reality He is the source of everything other than Himself. This God is both transcendent and immanent, above His creation and in it.

Atheism denies the existence of God. Agnosticism does not know, can never be sure. Deism, strong during the eighteenth-century Age of Reason, stressed God's transcendence, calling Him the Supreme Being who at one time had wound up the clock and now lets it run. Pantheism and its handmaid, romanticism, were more impressed with the immanence of God. God is all and all is God. The final destiny of everyone and everything is a melting into the Great-All, as creeks run into the rivers, and rivers flow into the seas.

Theism, however, makes a distinction between God and his creation. It is not necessarily the whole of the Christian conviction. We recall C. S. Lewis's conversion first to Theism and after that to a more personal faith in the God of revelation.

He makes that careful distinction in his autobiography: *Surprised By Joy.*

The Three Classic Arguments

Theism, using the approach of reason, has given us three significant arguments for the existence of God. It is worth discussing them before we move on to three more that have been posited. An evaluation of their importance and their inadequacy will round out this chapter.

The Cosmological. We find it used by Plato, Aristotle, and Aquinas. This argument implies a reasoning back to a final cause. Everything that exists must have a cause. Moving back from effects to causes which are effects of previous causes, reasoning from link to link of the chain, we must come to a First Cause which Aristotle called the Prime Mover.

The significance of this argument is that there must be some higher Power which is the source of all that exists. The inadequacy, however, is also apparent. For Aristotle the Prime Mover was the Unmoved Mover totally unconcerned about the creation and the creature. Such a Being cannot be approached by man except through a rational process. It is really only an idea revealing no love, no wise and kind providence, no redeeming concern. It is a far cry from the God of the Christian.

The Teleological. This is the argument from design. It reasons that there must be a directing Intelligence working towards definite ends. The eye, that first and most intricate camera, must have been planned and made by a greater Mind and for the purpose of seeing. The watch, that delicate instrument we so easily take for granted, was designed to tell time as accurately as possible. The entire universe and man, the one thinking creature in it as far as we know, exist, not by accident, but for a purpose that has blessedly plagued the mind for millenia. The sense of *telos,* or end, purpose, destiny, and destination will not down. Man seeks and posits a First Mind responsible for beginnings and their consummation.

The value of this argument is that it seeks an explanation of the universe and of life more satisfying than the conclusions of a mechanistic or materialistic philosophy. The weaknesses, however, are also apparent. Does reasoning from the example of the human mind necessarily lead to one Supreme Mind? Moreover, does it present us with only a Mind, not a Heart at the center of all that is? Again, how does one explain the presence of evil, pain, waste, and seeming purposelessness? Leibniz said that this is the best possible world, but Bertrand Russell among others sees no good or bad purpose in life but only final doom. And the gloomy existentialists speak of "the benign indifference of the universe."

The Ontological. This specifically *a priori* proof we owe to Anselm. "That than which no greater can be conceived" was the way he worded it. The inference is from the idea of God to His essence. No greater Being than God can be conceived, for if you could conceive of a greater Being, that would be God. The agreement of subjective thought and objective being must be caused by God Himself since no finite mind could conceive it.

The monk Gaunilo attempted to refute this proof by saying that one's idea of a perfect island does not convince anyone that such an island exists. But Anselm retorted that he was referring to *being* absolutely. An island exists only as a member of a class.

There is value in this argument. Descartes and Leibniz used it on this basis, that what the mind thinks is real. If this reasoning does not lead us to the assurance that there is a God, it may lead to a rationally coherent system of being. For man has the universe and his place in it as given, and he seeks the most reasonable account of both.

The ontological argument is basic to the other two we have mentioned. We must conclude, however, that all three arguments are useful but not sufficient. They show the strength of reason but also its limitations. There is a suggestion in what Trueblood says, that if God really is, one should expect the universe to proclaim Him.[1] He maintains that the Second Law of Thermodynamics points to Theism, for what is running down must have had a beginning. But in the last analysis faith is still basic to these proofs.

Speaking of these arguments or proofs Otto Pfleiderer writes: "They certainly cannot, and are not intended to engender the faith of the heart; yet they certainly serve the need of reason, which requires that faith be justified to thought."[2]

After a careful analysis of the arguments Herman Bavinck points out their inadequacy but concludes that they may serve as weapons for the believer who already believes in the God who reveals Himself in nature and in grace.[3]

Immanuel Kant, influenced by the scepticism of David Hume, rejected the classic arguments for the existence of God. In his *Critique of Pure Reason* he holds that a knowledge of God cannot be arrived at by the pure or speculative reason. The cosmological argument, stressing causation, applies only in a world of space and time. The teleological cannot prove a Creator-God. The ontological assumes what it is not able to prove, for existence is not a predicate. Reason deals only with phenomena, appearances; it cannot arrive at noumena.

Kant, convinced that pure reason was not the road to assurance, presented the practical or moral reason to clarify what religion implies.

The Moral Argument

In his *Critique of Practical Reason* Kant emphasized the genuine, moral imperative: "Du sollst," that is, "Thou shalt." Man has a conscience which is grounded in the deepest self and therefore in reality. When he says, "I ought," he has a moral experience which is a true revelation of the nature of reality. Such an experience has no meaning unless there is an objective moral order. That order is again meaningless unless there is a Divine Being who guarantees the good.

In the development of the moral argument Kant offers three postulates: God, Freedom, and Immortality.

The practical reason, therefore, reaches beyond the phenomenal into the noumenal to posit the God it requires. This is akin to the leap of faith, though Kant prefers to speak in terms of reason. With the lead the philosopher has given us we can go on asking what kind of God this would be. For Kant God is a presupposition essential to a moral order. But the practical reason leaves us still with a God-Idea rather than a personal God who reveals Himself in His Word and in the Word made flesh.

It was Matthew Arnold who described God as "a Power, not ourselves, that makes for righteousness." Such an abstraction deserves the sharp criticism of Francis Bradley in his *Ethical Studies*. If love without a lover is an absurdity, if the I-Thou relationship is at all important to human beings, it is not beyond the bounds of reason to expect God to be personal. The Christian is convinced that God's greatest revelation in Christ is very personal. However, it requires faith, which is more than practical reason, to accept this.

The second postulate is Freedom. Man as a moral creature has responsibility. He can deliberate and make decisions. He can choose between right and wrong. Such freedom is derivative, understandable if man is subject to a moral order underwritten by God. God then is the one who guarantees our best choices.

It is also true that the ultimate good cannot be attained in this life. Therefore, there must be a life hereafter. For that reason Kant presents his third postulate: Immortality. His practical reason requires an existence after this life. Human existence has its *finis*, its end, but it must also have its *telos*, its end as meaningful fulfillment, its destiny and destination. Life has its inferential; it seems to promise so much. Yet, it is also cut off, and we fly away. What more reasonable thought can there be than this, that if God is, man must also survive?

Kant has given us a rational argument, fascinating but not entirely convincing. What the pure reason cannot reach the practical reason assumes. It adds up to a natural theology and a significant but inadequate ethics of nature. The moral argument also falls short and needs desperately the givens of the Christian revelation.

The Evidence from History

Those who are aware of the soundings of contemporary theology notice that a shift has taken place from emphasis on ideas to emphasis on events. Adults in church school classes are studying *The Mighty Acts of God.*

Writers are not saying anything new when they remind us that God is active and working, but the added stress is significant. We hear of the logic of events in history. The Bible can be called the Acts of God. It was Horace Mann who once said, "I have never read of the resolutions of the apostles, but I have heard a great deal about the Acts of the Apostles."

All this adds up to evidence for the existence of God from historical experience.

As we have said before, the writers of the Bible do not have the philosophical approach. They record what God is doing, although they also listen to what He is saying, and that should not be forgotten.

The Word of God does reveal the great divine events, and the Apostles' Creed stresses them in verbs fully as important as the nouns.

It is true that the bee-hive activities of earth and the soaring events in space do not remind everyone of God. However, it is also true that for those with a religious bent there are thoughts which go beyond the farthest bounds of space. When Augustine wrote his *City of God,* he was fully aware of the Roman world and its civilization. But he saw within the City of Man and apart from it the City that has foundations, whose builder and maker is God. Convinced that the story of man is not the whole story, he believed that history is also a revelation of God's "one increasing purpose." For him, as for all Christian believers, the Eternal City will outlast all civilizations, fulfilling its divine destiny.

The evidence from historical experience, illumined by that special history of redemption in the Word, gives meaning to man's pilgrimage. However, it does so most effectively for those who believe in God as Creator, Providence, and Redeemer. For them the evidence is a valid form of the teleological argument.

The Evidence of the Religious Experience

When Saint Paul addressed the philosophers at Athens, he said, "I perceive that in every way you are very religious" (Acts 17:22b). The city was full of idols, including a marker to an unknown god.

Man is incurably religious. It may express itself in a respect for and fear of the unseen forces in and above nature, in the worship of many gods or one God. It may find satisfaction in the deification of self or human accomplishments. It may have more of the horizontal than the vertical, more of humanism than of theism, but the fact remains that man is a religious being.

It is reasonable not to dismiss this evidence lightly. Karl Marx speaks of religion as "opium," and the Communists smile sardonically at "pie-in-the-sky," but the religious experience, whatever it may be, is verified by millions of people who cannot be classified as deluded.

There is even something of scientific respect in regarding the highest form of religion as the most significant. That way Theism posits God, and the Christian theist, more specifically, believes in the God who reveals Himself in many ways but especially in His Word and in Jesus Christ, the most enlightening revelation.

To count it all delusion is as absurd as to smile away man's dreams about space before his achievements in space. There is much to be said for "the soul's invincible surmise," and there is more to be said about the religious experiences of an Isaiah, an Amos, the Apostles who met Christ in the flesh, an Augustine who sought and was found, a Pascal who stressed his need for a personal God, a Luther who defied the noise of solemn assemblies, a Calvin whose logic and burning heart were not at odds, a Wesley who counted the world as his parish, a Kierkegaard who linked suffering with love for God, a C. S. Lewis who was "brought in" kicking and struggling.

Reason alone will not explain the choice such men and countless others have made. The Christian faith is a mystery resolved only for those who have found by having been found, for those who have made the commitment to God, whose revelation illumines and changes the whole man.

The exclusive claims of Christianity fall on many deaf ears and shuttered hearts; but the evidence is there, and it is unreasonable to blink it away.

Like the other evidences the argument from the religious experience remains unconvincing before the bar of reason alone. But for those committed to the God of grace who has disclosed Himself in Jesus Christ and given the new birth through His Spirit it is very reasonable to believe in order that they may understand.

NOTES

1. Elton Trueblood, *Philosophy of Religion* (New York: Harper, 1957), p. 94.
2. Otto Pfleiderer, *The Philosophy of Religion* (London: Williams and Norgate, 1888), III, p. 254.
3. Herman Bavinck, *Gereformeerde Dogmatiek* (Kampen: J. H. Kok, 1908), II, pp. 60-74.

V

The Biblical View of God and Man

The idea of God has plagued man blessedly for millenia. Philosophers have given their views.[1] Scientists, stepping outside the field of facts, have given their conclusions. The average citizen has his notions, depending on what he believes or disbelieves.

Arthur Lovejoy, the late professor of philosophy at Johns Hopkins, was asked at one time if he believed in God. His reply was: "Which God?" It is said that he wrote thirty-three definitions. The implication is that philosophically he could come to no satisfactory conclusion.

Those who respect philosophy and science but prefer no substitute for the Scriptures also have a knowledge of God. Those men who wrote the Word received a revelation not found in nature and the universe, nor in unaided reason.

The Bible is a religious and moral book, not a scientific one. As Suzanne de Dietrich says, it speaks to us *in the name of* God, though I would question her statement that it does not speak to us *of* God.[2] To know God and to be known by Him is of vital importance, but to know about Him is also significant. God may be a great blur for many, but that is inexcusable in the light of the fact that He has revealed Himself to and through men who were inspired.

Because this revelation is with us, we have a right and a duty to be theologically scientific in gathering from it our knowledge of God. In the Word, God discloses himself in language and in events. In unfolding the Mighty Acts of God the Scriptures do so in language that requires careful consideration.

Knowing God in a personal way and knowing about Him are not identical, but knowing about Him can put content into one's faith. The emphasis today is away from propositional truth and leans heavily towards commitment and involvement. But you cannot have revelation without some propositional expression unless revelation means only a personal, mystical experience which the moment it is expressed becomes propositional. Even Tillich's description of God as the Ground of our Being is that.

We can understand the alarm voiced when knowledge about God takes the place of believing in Him. However, we can also be alarmed when the Word of God is deprived of its objective validity and authority and is considered the Word only when it comes to grips with the individual. We have no quarrel with its coming to grips with him. It certainly did that in the lives of those to whom the revelation came. But if what was revealed had not been recorded, what kind of revelation would we have, what would we know about God, and how could we know Him who sent Jesus Christ into the world, whom to know is life eternal?

The God who discloses Himself in the Bible is not the God of the philosophers but the God of Abraham, Isaac, and Jacob, as Pascal cries out in the *Pensées*. He is not just a Power, not "My Other Me" of the religious humanist, but as Jesus said, He is spirit and must be worshiped in spirit and in truth.

The God who makes Himself known in words and events is the Eternal One who created the universe with time, as Augustine states it. In Deuteronomy 33:27 we read: " 'The eternal God is your dwelling place, and underneath are the everlasting arms.' " Psalm 90, attributed to Moses, speaks with solemnity and beauty of Him who is from everlasting to everlasting. In Revelation 1:8a we read: " 'I am Alpha and Omega,' " the beginning and the end, the first and last. This concept of God does not seem to square with our ideas of time and space, but it is the believer's response of the whole man that comes to understanding.

The mystery of God implies an unfolding revelation. Isaiah could address Him as the God who hides Himself, meaning that man cannot comprehend Him. But apprehension is man's privilege and challenge. Revelation discloses that God is holy, infinite, independent, unchangeable, all-knowing, all-powerful, everywhere present, good, loving, righteous, truthful, and sovereign.

The names of God are very revealing. *Elohim* refers to the God who made the universe, controls the operations of nature, and rules in the affairs of men. *Jehovah* is the name of Him who made a covenant with His people, revealing His love and His judgment. *Father* is perhaps the most readily understood name. The fatherhood of God has two meanings. He is the Father of all people by virtue of creation; He is the Father in Jesus Christ of those who believe in Him.

The God of the Scriptures is an active, working God. He is the Creator of heaven and earth, having no desire to exist only for Himself. He planned and brought into being a reality besides Himself. It was His love expressing itself mightily. In that sense creation is also grace.

All that has been created is distinct from God, not an emanation as certain philosophers proposed. God is not to be identified with the world as pantheism maintains. Nor is He withdrawn from the world as the eighteenth-century deists held. He transcends all that He has made, yet is immanent in the world, nearer than hands and feet. As Paul says, those who believe in Him are temples of His Spirit.

Creation and the creature are not eternal. They were called into being. They were not, they are now in time, and they will not be in this form forever. The Word speaks of the new heavens and the new earth, the re-creation that is in store for us in the redemptive plan.

Calvin reminds us that the world is "the theater of God's glory." In such a world knowledge, history, faith, prayer, and miracles make sense. Man is not the victim of mechanical forces, nor of mysterious Fate or Fortune.

In the teaching of the Scriptures there is the clear note of a divine Providence that complements creation. God has a plan and a purpose. There is a teleology which gives meaning to all that is. This has escaped Bertrand Russell and our contemporary existentialists whose gloom sees only doom.

By divine Providence we understand that God preserves and governs all that He has created. Psalms like the 19th and the 104th express His presence in the universe, in nature, and in the mind and heart of man. The prophets speak of His ruling and overruling the nations. Jesus says that the divine eyes are upon the sparrow, and that the hairs of our heads are numbered. Hebrews 1:3 tells of God's ". . . upholding the universe by the word of his power. . . ." The Book of Revelation in poetic and figurative language sings of the final triumph of God's people and the ushering in of the new heavens and the new earth.

The Heidelberg Catechism expresses it beautifully and simply. By Providence is meant "The almighty and everywhere present power of God, whereby, as it were by His hand, He upholds and governs heaven, earth, and all creatures, so that herbs and grass, rain and drought, fruitful and barren years, food and drink, health and sickness, riches and poverty, yea, all things come not by chance, but by his fatherly hand."

There is also cooperation between God and man. Man must do his part in cultivating and appreciating the best that life has in store. However, he must acknowledge his dependence on God in whom we live and move and have our being as Paul said at Mars Hill. Always "God is at work in you both to will and to work for his good pleasure" (Philippians 2:13).

The teleology of creation and Providence require another act of God to make for fulfillment, and that is redemption. Fallen man who brought tragedy upon himself and the world needs that salvation which God alone can give. The Word of God presents that *Heilsgeschichte,* or Holy History, making clear the divine plan and purpose to restore man so that, in Milton's words, he may "regain the blissful seat." God called Abraham to be the father of a special people, the people of the Covenant whose gift to the world is the Old Testament. In that rich collection of books there is the forward look, the sure promise of a Redeemer.

In the New Testament there is the fulfillment. Jesus Christ, Son of God and Son of Man, the Word made flesh, whose glory we have beheld, is the awaited Messiah. According to His own words He and the Father are one, no one comes to the Father but by Him. He is the way, the truth, and the life. He lived, taught, healed, suffered, died, and rose again. As Cullmann says, He has given us D-Day and has assured us of V-Day.[3] The revealing "I-am" passages in the Gospel of John impress us with the fact that Jesus is a natural in the supernatural. No human being would dare to say what our Lord said about Himself.

This Jesus, after His ascension, poured out the Holy Spirit upon His Church on Pentecost Day. The Acts of the Apostles is the first chapter in the history of that Church. The rest of the New Testament emphasizes the Mighty Acts of God in and through His Church, and the final consummation in time and beyond.

Because we have the story of the world, the long history of man, and besides these, the divine revelation in the Word, we know that man is involved in a tale of two cities as Augustine develops it in his classic. The City of God is within the City of Man, yet above it. And the former will triumph because of God's one increasing purpose.

With all this evidence before us it is difficult to understand those who, like Bishop John A. T. Robinson, have let so much of Scripture pass through their intellectual sieves. Yet perhaps it is not so difficult, for if one allows reason to take over and faith to play a secondary role, the Word of God loses its infallible character as revelation.

The emphasis of Robinson and others on the Bible's presentation of the God of a three-story universe is heavily one-sided. A careful reading of the Scriptures makes clear that God was very real to Moses, the historians, the psalmists, and the prophets. He was transcendent, to be sure, but also immanent. Moreover, the God who personalized and concretized Himself in Jesus Christ came to the world through Bethlehem and Palestine, and sent His Spirit to work mightily in the Church and in individuals, never to leave them.

Throughout the Bible God is present with His people. The Word speaks of His essence but also of His existence, His engagement in history. John Courtney Murray, S. J., makes a case for God's words to Moses on the mount as implying "I shall be there as who I am shall I be there."[4] This is understood also in the name Immanuel, God with us. Essence and existence are complementary.

Others besides Nietzsche have proclaimed the death of God. There is the fool, the senseless man of Psalm 14. There are the calloused, godless people who fashion idols galore. There is the philosopher who makes the radical decision in favor of his reason. There is the Marxist revolutionary who considers God the enemy. There are the gloomy existentialists who strive for a questionable freedom which also issues in absurdity. And today there are the "God-is-Dead" theologians who, even when they are most charitably interpreted, disclose no desire to let the God of the living Word come alive again for this generation.

For all of them God is absent or dead. He is that, not only for millions who cannot or will not believe in Him, but also for those who, obsessed with man's coming of age, have no taste for the ageless revelation. Murray emphasizes his conviction that the will to deny God is the inspiration, not the conclusion, of their philosophy.

What is lacking, what is lost is faith as trust, commitment, and faithfulness, faith in the God who has made Himself known in His Word and especially in Jesus Christ, the Incarnate One.

The words of Isaiah 55:11 are still pertinent in this postmodern age: ". . . so shall my word be that goes forth from my mouth; it shall not return to me empty, but it shall accomplish that which I purpose, and prosper in the thing for which I sent it."

Man

Within the last decades theological thinking has been much concerned with the doctrine of man. This rebirth of interest is in part a wholesome response to the analysis of man in contemporary philosophy, literature, and the theater.

Man is the crown of creation as the first chapters of Genesis reveal and all Scripture implies. According to Herman Bavinck God realizes His purpose in creating man who was made to love, worship, and serve Him, and to understand the divine direction in all creation. The first chapter of Genesis gives a general history of creation, which finds its purpose and end in man. The second chapter deals in particular with the creation of man and the position in which the other creatures stand to man. In the first report man is the end of creation; in the second he is the beginning of history.[5]

One of the finest presentations of man in relation to God and the universe is given by the inspired poet of the 8th Psalm. The writer is neither philosopher nor scientist but a believer who responds with heart and mind to the divine revelation that is more than the fruit of his reflection. Within the framework of God the poet observes the heavens and asks what man is that God should be mindful of him and care for him. The immensity of the universe almost moves him to confess man's insignificance. Yet faith in God conquers. The Creator has made man a little less than God or the angels and has given him dominion over creation. Man is more than many sparrows and many planets.

Man is not lost in infinite space, nor does he dwindle into nothingness. The created world looms large, but as Pascal says, man knows more than the vast, immaterial universe. Emil Brunner writes: "Man is no more lost in this bigger universe which we know than he was when first tied to this world. Our dependence on God is not affected by the size of the mundane world. If we are overcome by fear because of the vastness of the universe, it is because we have the wrong standing ground. Man, created in and for the Word of God, whose self is the Eternal Son, is above the world. There is the 'saving history' which is not affected by bigness."[6]

These men speak in the vein of the psalmist, not overawed by the distant stars but moved by a faith in God who has not left man an orphan in the immensities.

At the heart of the doctrine of man lies the concept of the divine image in man. Scripture presents us with this all-important teaching, the meaning of which has been pondered by some of our best theologians. Their findings should help to clarify our understanding.

In the first volume of his *Dogmatiek* (I,1) Barth holds that the image of God in man is wholly lost as a result of the Fall; that there is no point of contact where God and fallen man meet; and that only in faith can there be a miraculous restoration of the image and the point of contact. But in the third volume of this work there is a change. There Barth no longer holds that man's existence in the image has been lost.[7] Man still remains man, and God recognizes him as such, though fallen and lost. However, only the man who is redeemed, who loves God and obeys His call is truly in the image. There is no restoration of the image except in and through Jesus Christ.

This view that the image of God in man has been terribly defaced by the Fall and can be restored only through salvation in Christ is also held by Calvin, Brunner, John Baillie, Bavinck, and Berkouwer. Principal Baillie gives a clear and satisfying presentation of the universal image in these words:

> It is thus possible to hold that the selfsame image of God, which by the power of Christ is restored in the souls of the saints, is to be found dimly and brokenly reflected in all human nature, behind and below the ravaging defacements

of sin's corruption; and at the same time to magnify to
the uttermost the implacably urgent need of the restoration itself, of the new creation and the new birth.[8]

Brunner cautions us as to "the dangerous and vague concept of the remnant of the image." He prefers to distinguish
between the formal and the material side of the image. The
formal is not lost, for man is still human and a responsible
being, a subject. There is still a point of contact which includes everything in man on which the Word of God takes
hold in order to give us faith. The universal or formal image
consists in man's standing before God as a responsible being
in the I-Thou relationship. This responsibility in love, the true
nature of man, is expressed not only to God, but also to our
neighbor.[9]

Brunner, however, maintains that the material image is
completely lost and can be restored only through Jesus Christ.

Cairns prefers to call the formal or universal image the
Old Testament image. He finds it referred to in James 3:9
and in Mark 12:16. He sees the New Testament image in
"Christ's perfect humanity, in which by faith men can share,
and in which they hope to be perfected."[10] The latter requires regeneration and faith.

For Calvin "the image of God constitutes the entire ex-
cellence of human nature as it shone in Adam before the
Fall." It is characterized by rectitude, the integrity of the
whole soul, and implies constant dependence on God and
obedience to His Word and will. Even in the body man reflects the image of God. Also the community of saints, having
a relationship to God and to one another, images the divine
glory.[11]

The image, however, was mutilated by the Fall and is now
tainted with impurity even in the elect. What is left is the
natural man's dim awareness of God although that is per-
verted from the beginning. Man naturally possesses the seed
of religion, and the distinction between good and evil is en-

graved on his conscience. In this respect the human race differs from all other creatures on earth.[12]

Calvin also insists that the divine image can be restored only through salvation in Christ who is the most perfect image of God.[13]

In several of his works Bavinck makes a careful study of the subject. In general his conclusions are similar to Calvin's. He speaks of the image in the broader and in the narrower sense. Originally it included a spiritual and bodily health which was indicated as knowledge, righteousness, and holiness, or original righteousness in accordance with Ephesians 4:24 and Colossians 3:10. As a result of sin man lost the image in the narrower sense but retained it in the broader sense. Man is still a rational, moral creature with whom God is concerned. Though sin damaged and spoiled the image in the broader sense, it did not destroy man and creation. By divine grace the hope of restoration was kept alive and made effective in the plan of redemption.

Bavinck maintains that flesh and spirit, body and soul partake of the image. Scripture does not look upon soul and body dualistically as the Neo-Platonists and the Manichees did. The whole man is in the image of God.[14]

The divine image is not limited to individual man. It is unfolded most fully in entire humanity, for it is much too precious to be realized in a single human being no matter how richly endowed.

It is only through the Incarnate Christ, who is the perfect image of God, that man and the creation can be restored.

Although Calvin warns against making man's lordship over creation the sum-total of man's likeness to God, Bavinck stresses the significance of man's dominion. For the divine mandate implies, not only God's will as to man's calling, but also the gracious qualification for that calling. As is evident from the creation story and the progressive revelation in the Scriptures man has both privilege and responsibility, the task

to cultivate and appreciate the best that life offers. In it all
he glorifies God and serves himself and his fellowman.[15]

If the reader has been disturbed by this brief summary of
a vast literature, the following conclusions as to the doctrine of
man should be clear.

Man is a created being. Made in the image of God, he is
endowed with reason, will, and emotions. As a moral creature
he had the freedom to choose right or wrong. His revolt
against his Maker brought on near-tragedy. Though the image
was tragically mutilated, he remained man. By divine grace
hope also remained, and the assurance of redemption on
God's terms was made plain in a far more concrete manner
than the story of Pandora's box ever implied.

We must now turn to a study of man's freedom within the
framework of the intriguing problem of evil.

NOTES

1. Cf. A. S. Pringle-Pattison, *The Idea of God* (New York:
   Oxford University Press, 1920).
2. Suzanne de Dietrich, *God's Unfolding Purpose* (Philadelphia: Westminster Press, 1960).
3. Oscar Cullmann, *Christ and Time* (London: SCM Press,
   1952), p. 84.
4. John Courtney Murray, S. J., *The Problem of God* (New
   Haven: Yale University Press, 1964), pp. 97 ff.
5. Herman Bavinck, *Gereformeerde Dogmatiek* (Kampen: J.
   H. Kok, 1908), II, pp. 543-544.
6. H. Emile Brunner, *Man in Revolt* (London: Lutterworth
   Press, 1939), chap. 18 especially.
7. See also David Cairns, *The Image of God in Man* (London:
   SCM Press, 1953).
8. John Baillie, *Our Knowledge of God* (New York: Oxford
   University Press, 1952), p. 102.
9. Cairns, *op. cit.*
10. *Ibid.* I, p. 35.
11. John Calvin, *Institutes* (Edinburgh: Clark), I, 15, 3, 4.

12. *Ibid.,* II, 2, 17, 18, and III, 7, 6.
13. *Ibid.,* I, 15, 4.
14. Bavinck, *op. cit.,* II, pp. 596, 601, 602.
15. See especially *Magnalia Dei* (Kampen: J. H. Kok, 1909), pp. 621, 622.

VI

The Problem of Evil

One of the most perplexing yet also most fascinating problems man faces is the one concerning evil. Man has wrestled with it for millenia. The concern is evident in an ancient Greek poem:

> Pity our eagerness to know
> Whence we have come, and whither go,
> How came into the world, and why,
> Sin, and her daughter, misery.

Sophocles wondered how the gods could be complacent about suffering and sorrow. Omar Khayyam found no answer with Doctor and Saint and proposed drowning it all in the juice of the grape.

An ancient Deva's song presents the perennial human predicament:

> We are the voices of the wandering wind,
> Which moan for rest, and rest can never find.
> Lo, as the wind is, so is mortal life —
> A moan, a sigh, a sob, a storm, a strife.

In "Dover Beach" Matthew Arnold, experiencing the throes of nineteenth-century doubt, sings of the sea of faith that once was at the full but now is ebbing with "its melancholy, long, withdrawing roar." And in "Stanzas From the Grand Chartreuse" he speaks of

> Wandering between two worlds, one dead,
> The other powerless to be born.

The presence of evil in the world has had its attractions, reactions, and explanations. Sorrow and trouble seem to intrigue us more than joy. The Greek tragedies are more impressive than Aristophanes. Shakespeare's tragedies are more gripping than his comedies. As Elton Trueblood reminds us, most popular songs are sad.

There are various reactions to the persistence of evil. One can be an optimist like Leibniz who considered this the best possible world; or like Browning's Pippa, who on her free day enjoys life to the full and sings:

> God's in his heaven —
> All's right with the world.

One can be a pessimist like Schopenhauer, who maintained that the very existence of the world is the greatest evil of all; or like Thomas Hardy, who ends *Tess of the D'Urbervilles* with the chilling words: " 'Justice' was done, and the President of the Immortals had ended his sport with Tess." The pessimism is evident also in the realistic novelists and dramatists of our century and in the despairing existentialists who see no light from beyond but cherish whatever spark there remains in the individual. An exhibition of some contemporary art is also a commentary on what man becomes when ideas and ideals are as lost as Atlantis.

One can be a meliorist who considers this world as neither worst nor best but getting better. Time was when evolution promised a gradual sloughing off of the ape and tiger. Good would be the final goal of ill, and that goal would be the Parliament of Man, the Federation of the World as Tennyson sang. Those who placed great hope in the social gospel were somewhat of that mind. However, after two World Wars and in the contemporary world setting with turmoil on every continent man may not be so sure.

Some Explanations

Grappling with the problem of evil, man has come up with challenging explanations.

Buddhism insists that evil is in the very nature of the world. There is the unrelenting law of Karma determining man's successive states of existence. The only hope lies in getting free from all desire and melting into Nirvana, an immortality like that of rivers flowing into the sea.

Persian dualism speaks of good and evil as light and darkness, two powers that have always been in conflict. This teaching also influenced Manicheism and Neo-Platonism, two religious-philosophical systems of thought in which Augustine floundered until he surrendered to the Christian revelation.

Socrates held that knowledge is virtue and ignorance is sin. Yet, though we are much indebted to the searching mind of this gadfly, we fail to find an emphasis on the will without which knowledge remains lefthanded. For to know the good requires also the will to do it if the good is to be accomplished.

Plato and after him the Gnostics, Manicheans, and Neo-Platonists held that evil has its origin and seat in matter. Matter and spirit are two opposing forces. It has always been so. In the *Theaetetus* we read: "Evil can never pass away; for there must always remain something which is antagonistic to good."

For Hegelianism evil is a necessary stage in the development of spirit. The Fall is considered a Fall upward, prophetic of man's striving and final triumph.

For Augustine, the Christian, evil is the negation or privation of the good. It has no real essence. It was not created. It is an intrusion. God permitted evil in order to bring about good.

These explanations, all our rational explanations, inevitable as they may be, fall short. For man knows nothing about origins by reason alone.

This is not saying that man should cease thinking about

the problem. Martineau insists that we would have to re-
nounce reason if we are to be "saved from tears." But we
would add that the best approach to understanding is from the
point of view of man's wholeness. Man is a rational, religious,
and moral being. He pays a price for being human, and at
his best he prefers it that way. As human he is not alone.
There is a higher reference. There is a God who has revealed
the way which leads beyond evil and beyond tears.

We must believe that there is a God who wills the absolute
good. Strictly speaking, the problem of evil arises only when
belief is intense and urgent. What can the unbeliever, who
does not accept God, or who blames the God in whom he will
not believe, really say? Or again, how can one argue against
the indifference of the universe or a deterministic system?

In order to come to an understanding of our problem we
must believe in a personal God who treats us as persons. As
Berdyaev says, "The evil of the world presupposes the existence of God, without it, it would be impossible to get to know
him."[1] A personal God must honor persons in their wholeness
here and in the life to come.

Before we study what the Word says about the problem of
evil, we must treat briefly several proposed solutions in some
of which the reality of God is a significant factor.

Five Proposed Solutions

We owe a debt to Elton Trueblood for crystalizing five
answers to the problem of why there can be evil in a world
that God made.[2] Wherever it is necessary we shall add to his
critique.

The first solution, which Trueblood treats secondly, is that
evil is an illusion. This is held by Christian Science and some
versions of absolute idealism. However, we are only duping
ourselves if we hold to this theory, for evil is much too real,
too actual in our lives. How does the "illusion" of wickedness,

pain, suffering, arise? Would it not also be a real, unexplain-
able evil?

Moreover, if all evil is swallowed up by the Absolute, as
some idealists hold, there is small comfort in contemplating
such an impersonal reservoir. Besides, what would be the
moral challenge in contending against an illusion? A far better strategy would be to ignore it.

Another solution proposed is that evil is a necessary defect
in a good plan. As darkness is essential to light, as ugliness
sets off beauty, so evil provides an antagonism that is to the
advantage of good. But we may well ask how much evil is
necessary. Could we not do with less? And is it fairly dis-
tributed? In a world of evil and suffering it is easy enough to
say, "Keep your fingers crossed," or "Keep your chin up," but,
to quote Trueblood:

> The toad beneath the harrow knows
> Exactly where each tooth-point goes;
> The butterfly, upon the road,
> Preaches contentment to the toad.

We think also of the line from *Romeo and Juliet*: "He jests
at scars who never felt a wound."

It is true that we learn from the conflict of opposites, and
that we can be strengthened for the good by antagonisms, but
how much of evil is essential, and how fair should the distribution be? Moreover, this solution throws no light on the
origin of evil.

A third answer is that evil is a limitation of God's power.
This presupposes a finite God, not as to goodness or intent,
but as to power. The solution is far too drastic, and it leaves
us with a host of problems. If God is limited, can He be God?
Is there a force greater than Himself under whom or which
He must serve? There is a recurring question. If there is so
much evil in the world, how did man ever come upon the idea
of a good God?

A fourth solution, more challenging, is found within the

framework of divine revelation. It is that suffering is the direct result of a specific sin, and a just recompense. We recall two dramatic examples in the Bible.

Job's friends accused him of some secret sin for which he was suffering, for the Almighty would not let a good man down. The easy answer did not satisfy Job, nor does it satisfy us. No particular sin had brought on his calamity. Neither Job nor his friends understood the divine testing. The Voice from the whirlwind gave an answer, but it was not the answer reached by the rational quest to justify the ways of God to man.

There are two passages in the Gospels dealing specifically with this proposed solution. In Luke 13:1-4 Jesus asks if those Galileans who were slain by Pilate at their sacrifices and those eighteen on whom the tower of Siloam fell were greater sinners than those who were not the victims. In John 9, which tells the story of the healing of the blind man, the disciples ask if it was this man's sin or his parents' sin that caused the blindness. Jesus' reply is that the man's misfortune is not the result of a particular sin. However, the works of God would become evident in the healing.

Years ago Thornton Wilder dealt with the problem in *The Bridge of San Luis Rey*. A primitive bridge in Peru over which people had passed for more than a century suddenly collapsed, hurling five people into the deep gorge. Was it just an accident, or was there something in the lives of these individuals that led to the calamity? The author delves into the past of each of them. But the answer is not forthcoming as it is not for any who propose the solution we are discussing.

It is true that some sins bring their reward, that man reaps what he sows. The criminal, the drunkard, the person who neglects his health, the careless driver, the loveless egoist often meet their just reward. However, there are other instances in which reference to a just recompense is out of order.

We are still perplexed by the prosperity of the wicked as Asaph was in Psalm 78, until from the divine perspective we see the judgment that is inevitable. We are more perplexed by the suffering and death of a little child, by some promising life nipped in the bud, by the plight of our friends in hospital beds and wheel chairs while we walk with a bounce. The victims of wars, tornadoes, earthquakes, floods, and pestilence are more than news items. Their plight arouses our compassion and urges us to help them. It should also move us to ask the honest question: "Were these more guilty than we are?" To which Jesus would answer, "No."

The fourth solution is far too general and too superficial to satisfy the earnest questioner.

There is a solution, however, which appeals to those who have the conviction that the whole man is related to God who made him. It is the answer of childlike faith. The rationalist, the naturalist, the humanist, the positivist will brush it aside as irrelevant; but the believer finds in it comfort and assurance and even a measure of explanation.

Turning to Job again we see a man who never loses his hold on God. He has patience at times as James states in his Epistle. But he is also a stormy petrel challenging the Almighty to dialogue. At first he expresses the resignation of faith. "The Lord has given, and the Lord has taken. Blessed be the name of the Lord." Then he despairs of his life, becomes angry with his friends, and pleads for understanding. He reaches the high water mark of his faith when he cries out, "I know that my Redeemer lives." And that Redeemer will justify His cause.

Job and his friends have indulged in a cascade of words. They are not prepared for the startling answer from the Voice out of the whirlwind. The speeches of the Lord are not aimed at satisfying man's curiosity but at reminding man of His creatureliness. Job is overawed by the majesty and greatness of the Almighty who is the All-Loving as well. For God has tested His servant Job and has not forsaken him. He also reprimands the friends who have not spoken right.

The saints of Scripture at their best trust in God no matter what befalls. They may cry out as in the *De Profundis,* they may at times wonder if God has forgotten grace, they may smart under judgment, but for them God is not lost in a three-story universe. God is near and is willing to reason with them as Isaiah has it. His promises are sure, and His judgments may not be trifled with.

Jesus promised His followers a hard road. He sent them out as sheep among wolves. In the world they would have tribulation. He did not always take away the thorn as Paul experienced, but He gave them a cross and the command to follow him. Their faith did not remove all perplexities. Their all-too-human reasoning, like ours, found no itemized clarifications. But the discipline which evil and suffering bring stood them in good stead. By grace they kept the faith, and it kept them.

Though faith is the final answer, it is well to be humble before mysteries. We are not alone in our perplexities; and it is the part of wisdom to shun easy answers.

Light From the Word

It is to revelation that we must turn for the most satisfying solution to our problem. For God in His self-disclosure both in words and deeds has much to tell us about origins, purpose, and destiny.

From the inspired Word we learn that God is holy and just. He cannot be, He is not the source of evil. Though it may not satisfy the ultra-predestinarian, perhaps the best we can say is that God willed it in the sense that He permitted it. But He also uses and overrules it.

It is evident from Scripture that evil existed before the Fall of man. There are references to the Devil, or Satan, the Adversary. In Genesis 3:1 he appears in the form of a serpent to tempt Eve and Adam. In the book of Job he appears in the council of heaven and is permitted to harass God's servant. Jesus is tempted by him in the wilderness. Our

Lord took demons and demon possession seriously. He was not just a child of His times accepting a common belief. On the contrary He challenged and defeated the enemy on many occasions.[3]

In I Peter 5:8 we read of the Adversary prowling about as a roaring lion, seeking to devour whom he can. In the Book of Revelation he is pictured as the dragon who causes woe upon woe and is finally cast into the bottomless pit.

From the Word we gather that God created spirits to do His bidding. Some of these rebelled and were cast out of heaven. In Timothy 3:6 a man aspiring to the office of bishop is warned against the pride which caused the condemnation of the Devil. And in II Peter 2:4 we are told that God did not spare the angels who sinned, but cast them into hell.

We must never confuse Milton with Scripture, but his description of the fall of the angels in his epic, *Paradise Lost,* is tremendously impressive.

From the limited references in Scripture we gather that there was a rebellion in the spirit world. How can it be explained? The evil deed is the result of the evil will, but what is the origin of the latter?

The most appealing explanation is that God desired a moral universe in which His creatures were given the freedom to choose between good and evil. That held for angels and also for man.

God created man a spiritual, moral, responsible personality with freedom of choice. He made him "able not to sin"; he did not create him "not able to sin." Wherever there is personality, there is moral choice.

The tragic fact is that man chose wrongly. His transgression was an act of self-will. In attempting to become independent he was false to his true position as creature. This was the Fall that brought on "loss of Eden and all our woe."

The rebellion of man, an act of pride, affected the entire human race. Evil is the high price man paid for moral freedom. The doctrine of original sin implies that we are all involved. However you may debate it or define it, there is a blight on us from our birth. Even Harry Emerson Fosdick in one of his sermons speaks of "a racial inheritance rolling down from generation to generation, ruining all the fair hopes of man."

In this connection it is interesting to note what T. E. Hulme, a brilliant literary personality of the early twentieth century, wrote about original sin. Writing from a perspective that is non-Biblical and non-evangelical, he accuses philosophy and romanticism of failure to grasp the significance of the doctrine of original sin. Whatever he writes he considers prolegomenous to Pascal.[4]

In spite of the explanation given by Scripture the question still persists why God permitted evil. Why did He not kill the Devil? We hear it in this form today: "If God is good, why does He allow so much misery?"

Again the answer from the Word is that God made a moral universe in which man as a moral being had the freedom to choose. God treats him as a personality, not as a robot nor as a child tied in the cellar to keep him from harm. God's love persuades; it does not tyrannize.

Moreover, the whole history of redemption and the triumph of grace recorded in the divine revelation proves that God wanted rectitude, not rebellion. His desire has always been to restore man. That is why He promised a Redeemer. That is why His Son came into the world to minister, to suffer, to die, and to rise again. Calvary trumpets the love and the justice of God. He takes guilt and sin very seriously. Faith in Jesus Christ saves man and lifts him beyond tragedy.

In the Word, evil and sin are faced squarely. There is no speculation, but a recognition of man's tragic situation. There is definitely the revelation of how this can be overcome. And always we find the strong emphasis on the responsibility of man in the presence of salvation and judgment.

C. S. Lewis says, "The road to the Promised Land leads

past Sinai." For the believer it leads through the vale of suffering which becomes and will more fully become the desert blossoming like the rose.

The Christian is promised the resurrection and the new heavens and the new earth. That is why he can view evil and suffering from a far different perspective than that of the persistent critic who fails to accuse himself.

The Christian of today, like the saints of old, trusts in God who will not let him drift beyond his love and care. He has the final answer as we have described it, but not every answer to every question. He too may at times still ask, "Why?," remembering that even Jesus on the Cross asked it. He cannot fully explain what we call natural evils, calamities that fall upon some either individually or collectively. He cannot explain all suffering, nor why he escapes much of it. He does know that natural laws carry through. Water and fire may be helpful or destructive. It is implied in a stable environment that has neither pity nor malice.[5]

The believer is assured that suffering can be redemptive. With Baron van Hugel he can say that even though Christianity does not explain suffering, it does show us what to do with it. There are shining examples of those who in their afflictions do not curse but show courage and gratitude. The molding of character often requires the anvil. What the easy life cannot give us the life of faith through struggle to triumph can.

NOTES

1. *Philosophy of Religion,* George L. Abernaethy and Thomas A. Langford, eds. (New York: Macmillan, 1962), p. 451. See also Nicholas Berdyaev, *The Beginning and the End* (New York: Harper, 1952), chap. V.
2. Elton Trueblood, *Philosophy of Religion* (New York: Harper, 1957), chap. 17.
3. See John James, *Why Evil?* (Baltimore: Pelican Books, 1960), chap. 3. Also Denis De Rougemont, *The Devil's Share*

(New York: Pantheon Books, 1944), and C. S. Lewis' *The Screwtape Letters* (New York: Macmillan).
4. T. E. Hulme, *Speculations* (London: Routledge and Keagan Paul, 1936).
5. John James has an interesting discussion on human solidarity, *op. cit.*, pp. 42 ff.

VII

The Meaning of History

What is history?

The very asking of the question indicates that the intelligent mind sees meaning, value, purpose in events and even in the words that describe these. We cannot get away from interpretations though these may vary widely.

For the student compelled to take courses history may be a textbook and collateral reading. For the average citizen it may appear a passing parade, of interest only to the specialist. For a few it is "bunk," or a chain of facts too long to memorize and too dry to be challenging. For the scholar it may be one or more of many things, depending on his point of view.

A Variety of Meanings

The Greeks had the cyclical view of time. For them history repeated itself. The Greek historians present us with facts and myths but do not give us an insight into the scheme of things. We must turn to their tragedians for a grappling with the human problems under the aspect of Fate and the gods. We appreciate Greek philosophy, especially that of Plato who in his *Republic* gives us his dream of the ideal state, and in other of his *Dialogues* shows his and Socrates' concern for immortality and judgment. Yet, whatever of the universally human is evident in this thinking, it requires more of a comprehensiveness which takes up the whole human drama, also of those "barbarians" who made up and make up the rest of the world.

Any interpretation of history is influenced by the perspective with which one begins, by the presuppositions with which one surveys the vast field or stream. The Zoroastrians looked upon life and the world as the eternal battleground between light and darkness. The Buddhist looks upon it all as illusion. Man can escape the hurt of existence only through contemplation and final "extinction" in Nirvana. The Hindu sees life as an endless round of reincarnations, and only oblivion brings relief from the interminable revolutions of the wheel.

Even Arnold Toynbee, who has put religion back into history and has drawn violent criticism for the attempt, propounds a cyclicism in which the four great religions and the author's syncretism play a significant role. He attempts to improve on the old cyclical interpretation of history by likening history to a wagon. The wheels go round and round, but in the meantime the conveyance moves forward. Whether the figure is more interesting than convincing will depend on the reader's acumen and on what his ideas of progress are.[1]

What then is history? Is it only a long chain of events with or without purpose? Is it a squirrel cage in which man goes round and round like the music in a popular song? Was Buckle right in emphasizing climate, soil, and food? Was Carlyle correct in presenting the Hero as the shaper of history? Or was Tolstoy nearer the truth when in *War and Peace* he stressed circumstance on the waves of which some person is lifted to temporal prominence? Is the Marxian position of economic determinism the whole story, or are there other important factors? Has religion anything to do with history, or is it quite negligible as Charles and Mary Beard's *The Rise of American Civilization* and *America in Midpassage* and Parrington's *Main Currents in American Thought* seem to imply?

Is history to be explained only on the horizontal level, or is there a transcendental reference? Some among us today may be satisfied with Thucydides' emphasis on natural causes, or Herodotus' stressing of chance, or Thomas Hill Green's infatuation with the people. Some may be satisfied with the vague assurance of progress, leaving it to evolution to work it out. Some will be comforted by the "American Dream," whatever that may promise. Others, and there are many of them, are assured that Communism is the last best hope of earth, promising a proletarian paradise of chrome and stainless steel. There the lambs can nibble at steel shavings with no fear from the capitalist lion who will be dead. In the light of the Party's ruthlessness this implies a rather naive doctrine of man.

What then is the meaning of history? Certainly it is events, but more than that, it is also thought and words concerning events. When a child is born, parents are not stricken dumb for the rest of their lives because they fear that the event may be spoiled by "meaningless" words. That is what some thinkers, even theologians, seem to imply when they magnify events and the activities of God, relegating words about events and even those words that give us the Word to a secondary place.

There is an interpretation that honors events and also the words which tell us of them, that honors the God who speaks in both words and events. This God ushered in the once-for-all Event that alone gives history meaning. To a study of that interpretation we now turn.

The Christian Interpretation

Even as it is rather banal to say that one religion is as good as another, so it is absurd to hold that one perspective as to history is as good as another. There is a radical difference between Gibbon's *The Decline and Fall of the Roman Empire* and Augustine's *City of God*. The eighteenth-century historian in his stately and meticulous chapters gives scant praise to the Christian movement. The fifth-century churchman presents us with the first Christian philosophy of history. It is a tale of two cities in which the City of God in the midst of the City of Man moves on to ultimate triumph.

There is a vast difference between Spengler's pessimism in *The Decline of the West* and Emile Cailliet's buoyant conviction that this universe is a great signaling station, the meaning of which we Christians must make out. "Our sovereign God, the Creator and Upholder of the universe, is at the roaring loom of events and reveals himself in his creation in the very texture of history, and in the human soul."[2]

Any point of view has something of a basic "bias" or "prejudice" in its stance. The Christian begins with the conviction that divine revelation and faith in the God who discloses Himself and His plan and purpose are essential to a proper understanding of history. That way history, far from being a mere chronicle of events, appears as a becoming shot through with purpose and direction, destiny, and destination. It is God's telling story of purposeful Creation, wise and kind Providence, and assured Redemption from tragedy. It is the history of divine grace and judgment, the impelling drama which unfolds our human pilgrimage through suffering to glory.

The story has been called *Heilsgeschichte,* or holy history. Otto Piper describes it in these words: "Holy history is not one of the many departments or periods of history, it is their heart and hidden center, and all other history moves, although it may be more or less unaware of this fact, in its orbit."[3]

This history, which we know from the revelation in the Word, is not like an elevated track above the street level of other history, but within the history of the world. We might compare it to a gulf stream, distinct from, yet present and effective in its influence on ocean and continents. It is there "to be recognized, understood, tested, and actualized." Related to world history as a whole, "it is the center and key to all events."[4] It is this because God is its Sovereign Lord. In

His Word He has made His purpose known in words and events.

The Hebraic-Christian tradition does not only have a history; it is history. A look at the narrative rewards us with a succession of events that have "a local habitation and a name."

It is the story told of a people and by a people, not speculative, but filled with reverence for God. At their best they held that "the fear of the Lord is the beginning of wisdom." This fear, properly understood, meant for them, not the cringing of a slave scourged to dungeon or galley, but reverence and awe, and the spirit of worship.

The Word begins with God who is, not with an idea about Him. It moves swiftly to a telling about Creation, man's Fall, and his Redemption.

God speaks and acts in calling Abraham, who is to be the father of a special people, the seed in whom all the nations of the earth will be blessed. With Abraham and his people God makes a covenant. He will be their faithful God, and they must be His loyal people. If they break their solemn vows, judgment is imminent. Far from being pampered, they have been elected *from* the rest of the peoples *for* carrying out God's holy purposes. Privilege was theirs, but also responsibility. Loyalty and obedience were demanded of them. Not on equal terms with God, always remembering their creatureliness, they were marked at their best by the full acknowledgment of God as God. This distinguished them from their contemporaries.

God made them a closely-knit people under Moses who received the Law by which their lives were to be guided. Constantly they were reminded that their God had brought them out of Egypt, out of the house of bondage. God gave them judges, and kings, and poets who sang for sheer joy or out of the depths of despair. And He sent them prophets who advised them and warned them of mercy and of judgment.

It was their disobedience that brought drastic measures.

The Bible, presenting the highest ideals for man, is also a realistic book. In the divine self-disclosure mercy and judgment go hand in hand. The prophets pleaded: "Come now, let us reason together, says the Lord: though your sins are like scarlet, they shall be as white as snow . . ." (Isaiah 1:18). They thundered that the wayward people should hearken unto the voice. They cried for repentance, for a return to God. The Almighty, tired of their empty sacrifices, reminded them that He had showed man what was good, and that He required of them justice, and loving kindness, and a humble walking with Him (Micah 6:8).

It is a breath-taking fact that whereas poets and sages in other nations often flattered their native countries, Israel's prophets repeatedly scourged their people.

The judgment fell. The chosen people, inwardly rebellious and politically divided, were led into captivities from which only a remnant returned. That remnant rebuilt Jerusalem and the Temple from which the glory had departed.

For a time they won their independence under the stalwart Maccabees, only to become subject to Rome. Where was the promise and the fulfillment?

The story, however, was far from ended. The forward look of the Old Testament, inspired by the promise of a Redeemer, was not doomed to failure. Already in Jeremiah 31:31-34 the Lord had promised the making of a new or renewed covenant that would apply, not only to the Jews, but to all the spiritual seed of Abraham. The coming of Jesus Christ, the Messiah, brought the promise to fulfillment. It was the once-for-all Event by which the whole of history was changed.

In the coming of Jesus Christ God acted decisively in a unique event and series of events. It is the words in the inspired Word which tell us of this divine break-through. Oscar Cullmann puts it well when he reminds us that Jesus' coming, his death, and resurrection imply the decisive battle, the D-Day which presages V-Day. The historical mission of Israel has been handed over to the new fellowship in Christ, his Church. The New Testament presents the Gospel, the Good News for which the world should have been waiting as people wait for the sunrise.

History, then, has its center in Jesus Christ, the Lord of history. It is by special revelation that we know this. God is the Lord of time, and Christ is the turning point. "Think him and all he said away, and history falls apart; it loses its heart, kernel, center; it becomes chaos."[5]

It is, therefore, the divine grace, revealed to us in the Word and especially in Christ, the Word made flesh, that assures us of the meaning of history.

"In Christianity there appears a history of humanity, a development which proceeds from a definite point and moves towards a definite goal, a progress towards an absolute ideal, towards true being, and eternal life. History becomes a drama which leads through suffering to glory, a *divina comedia* that reveals the slow but certain realization of the Kingdom of God and casts over this somber earth the splendor of the divine glory."[6]

"Apart from me ye can do nothing" (John 15:5c). These simple words of our Lord should cause us to pause and think. All His words and the Word which is His, and all His activities culminating in His death and resurrection, His ascension and pouring out the promised Spirit should remind us of what He has done to history and within it.

The New Testament, almost in breathless haste, tells us of the march of the Christian faith, of Christians who turned the world upside down or rightside up. The Church and the Kingdom were here to stay. They made their impact on the Roman Empire in which the seeds of decay were already at work. In his *City of God* Augustine traces that holy history which impinges on world history, acts as a leaven, and comes to ultimate triumph.

In following chapters we shall deal with the Church and with the Doctrine of the Last Things, both of which are very much in the news today. What is important for us in this chapter as in this entire book is the conviction that God is the Sovereign Lord of history who gives the answers to our questions in His Word, in events, and above all in the Event of Jesus Christ. ". . . God was in Christ reconciling the world unto himself . . ." (II Corinthians 5:19). Revelation comes to us "with its central idea of divinity made incarnate in a personality more human than the human one."[7]

Jesus Christ, rejected by His people, condemned and crucified under Pontius Pilate, is the heart of the matter for us who believe in His name. We date our years from His birth, but better still we attribute our rebirth to His grace. Because He makes the great difference in our lives, He provides the great difference in our perspective as to history. It is perhaps futile to speculate on what would have happened if He had not come. It is far wiser to acknowledge that He has come. Someone has suggested that when we feel inclined to ask what the world is coming to, it is far better to remind ourselves of what or who has come to the world.

We admit that our convictions are a "bias", a point of view we have chosen. It might, however, be better to say that it is a point of view that has chosen us. To know about God and Jesus Christ is one thing; but to know God in Jesus Christ and to be known by Him, that is something else. There is a *mystery* about salvation, but as the word implies there is also a continuing revelation. To come to an understanding requires a personal faith.

We believe in order that we may understand.

NOTES

1. See Arnold Toynbee's *A Study of History* (New York: Oxford University Press, 1940), and *Civilization on Trial* (Cleveland: Meridian, 1948).
2. *The Christian Approach to Culture* (New York: Abingdon-Cokesbury, 1953), p. 77.
3. Otto Piper, *God in History* (New York: Macmillan, 1939), p. XVI.

4. Karl Barth, *Church Dogmatics, a Selection* (New York: Harper Torchbooks), pp. 78, 94.
5. Herman Bavinck, *Wijsbegeerte Der Openbaring*, (Kampen: J. H. Kok, 1908), p. 119.
6. Herman Bavinck, *Verzamelde Opstellen* (Kampen: J. H. Kok, 1921), p. 107.
7. Herbert Butterfield, *Christianity and History* (New York: Scribner, 1950), p. 157.

VIII

Christian Faith and Science

It is possible that the repeated use of the phrase "knowledge explosion" has dulled our senses a bit "as though of [science we] had drunk." We understand that the words refer especially to man's dizzying progress in the fields of physics and chemistry and their related brood. Man has gotten beyond "the desire of the moth for the star," beyond the lure of sea and mountain. For centuries his eyes have been fixed on stars and planets, but he will not rest until his feet stand in the dust of Mars and the moon.

This is what science has done to man because he has done much with science. What has been accomplished in the last few decades seems to merit the description of an explosion. What the end results of the great adventure will be no one dares to predict, for man has an insatiable urge to know.

The mysterious universe still has many secrets, factual and spiritual. Many have been revealed; many more will be. If man will only keep in mind that facts are not the whole of knowledge, that interpretations, ideas, ideals, and faith are also essential to his true humanity, he will value that true humility which is one of the doors to understanding. Always remembering his creatureliness, appreciating and cultivating the descriptive sciences, he will do well also to consider the realm of values and to come to grips with all that religion implies.

Much has been said and written about the conflict between science and religion. What is really meant by the age-old problem? Is the tension somewhat relieved in our day? The answers require first of all an evaluation of the natural sciences.

The Significance of Science

The method of the natural sciences includes observation, description, prediction, calculation, verification, experimentation, and control. On the basis of what is learned hypotheses are made, and these again can be altered as new evidence appears. The method is inductive rather than deductive. Francis Bacon, rebelling against the generalization of Aristotelian philosophy, stressed the need for a careful examination of the object. Galileo calculated from what the telescope revealed. Darwin collected data before he drew his conclusions. Our contemporary scientists, drawing on all the complexities of their skills, spend years in the laboratory before sending up those space ships that astound us.

The urge to gain exact knowledge is commendable. The flowers which I plant and tend mean more to me after the botanist has informed me. The birds whose plumage and song delight me are more than a happy interruption when the ornithologist has had his say. The liquids and gases, essential to existence, or destructive, mean more when the chemist has unleashed or curbed them. Mechanics, heat, light, and sound, electricity and magnetism, radiation, and energy unlock their secrets through the physicist's experimentation. So also the astronomer, geologist, mineralogist, meteorologist, and archaeologist add more than information to the store of our knowledge.

The challenge of the sciences is there. Religion must accept the facts whenever these are established, for truth is truth wherever we find it. As Young says, "The Christian realist has no quarrel with the findings of science. For the Christian all truth is God's truth and should be accepted as such."[1]

Because much has been made of the conflict between science and religion, something should be said about the debt science owes to Christianity.

Herman Bavinck honored the natural sciences and maintained that each of these must have a certain independence and should not be dictated to by any of the others, nor by philosophy and theology.[2] Empirical knowledge is of the highest importance; it is a first step to scientific knowledge.[3]

The Dutch theologian stresses the point that Scripture does not teach a dualism between the natural and the spiritual. In general, Christianity has been a blessing for science, for research in nature. Science does not owe everything to Christianity because it springs from creation rather than from re-creation. But Christianity, offering the comfort to live and to die happily, works upon the whole man, upon his entire life, upon all his thinking and acting, and in that way it influences the development of the natural sciences.

Although the Middle Ages never dreamt of the advances of the natural sciences evident in our day, their emphasis on scholarship paved the way.

The Reformers also showed a great appreciation of nature as a revelation of God's glory, and many scientific men were Christians. The Reformation freed the individual for the task of answering to his calling and making all natural life sacred as service to God.

In the eighteenth century the emphasis on reason brought about a cleavage between the natural and the spiritual. In the nineteenth century the natural sciences blossomed amazingly, and in the twentieth their progress has been astounding. The breach between these and the religion of revelation still exists, although there is a growing evidence of understanding and compatibility.

Other scholars have expressed convictions similar to Bavinck's. John Baillie writes, "It is quite clear to me, then, that modern science could not have come into being until the ancient pagan conception of the natural world had given place to the Christian."[4] He quotes Nicholas Berdyaev as saying that Christianity alone made both positive science and technics possible. He refers to John Macmurray's statement that modern science is not only "the product of Christianity but its most adequate expression."[5] He reminds us of Friedrich van Hugel's emphasis on the need science and religion have for each other, and tells us that Bacon, Descartes, Copernicus, Gassendi, Galileo, Kepler and many other great seventeenth-century men held that the world was under God's guiding hand.[6]

This evidence may seem to clash with the obtuseness of the Church in accepting the givens of science. Stories of Galileo and Servetus come to mind. We must not confuse, however, the main drive of Christianity with the errors of Christendom.

The Limitations of Science

It would perhaps be better if we speak of the limitations of man, for science as exact knowledge, and revealed religion, concerned about the supernatural as well as the natural, need not ultimately be at odds.

Man is more than a scientist. He has emotions, will, imagination, and a measure of faith. He has his dreams, his ideals as well as his ideas. He is overawed by oceans and deserts and mountain peaks and more so still by the silent universe that almost engulfs him. He may spend a great part of his life glued to microscopes and telescopes, working with laboratory equipment, studying the life of bees and birds, and fashioning space craft, but he is first of all a man, perhaps a lover, a father and husband, who looks upon the members of his family as far more than specimens. He can have some kind of faith which leaps beyond the accomplishments of mind and hand. If it is the Christian faith, he has a sense of the divine molded by that revelation which offers both knowledge and experience.

Essential though it is, science does not satisfy the wholeness of man. Its purpose is to describe. When it begins to evaluate, it is no longer strictly science. This is where the harm often occurs, where the conflict arises.

To draw conclusions from the givens of science is certainly permissible, but the admission should also be made that this is no longer "pure" science. If an astronomer concludes from his observations that man is negligible, he is philosophizing beyond the bounds of the exact sciences; he is devaluating man, who after all is the astronomer. Moreover he is not recognizing other areas of knowledge and experience that could enlighten him.

Here lies the danger of that phrase often heard — "the scientific outlook." Strictly speaking science produces no outlook. The outlook springs from the urge in man to evaluate: but the evaluation deals with quality rather than with quantity or measurement.

This proves that man is concerned with more than physical matters. At his best he is also interested in final causes. The Pre-Socratics indulged in their own way in science, but the Socratics saw purpose in physical nature and applied themselves to the search for meanings. Christianity, guided by a greater revelation, acknowledges and thrives on the divine purpose in life, and strives for a better synthesis of the natural and the spiritual. A universe without meaning or purpose would negate much or all of what the sciences provide. Science without religious and moral insights can so easily produce a Frankenstein monster to terrify man and bring on annihilation.

The Greeks feared *hubris* or pride, recognizing the wrath of the gods. We in our day do well to remain humble in the face of man's incredible accomplishments, always remembering that the battle is not to the strong, nor the race to the swift, but that victory is for those who trust in Him who offers us both nature and grace.

There are other sciences besides those we usually call the natural ones. The Christian with scientific as well as religious interests appreciates all knowledge. He recognizes the gap between science and faith and the perennial conflict; but he also seeks understandingly to bridge the gap. He perceives that the conflict is not simply between believer and unbeliever, but that the man of faith and the man of science may be the same man experiencing the tension.

For example H. H. Price in a lecture delivered at Cambridge University says, "I do not see how any scientific argument could prove that physical space is the only space there is."[7] He goes on to say that no scientific discovery can disprove the existence of other worlds and of God.

So also Karl Heim in a difficult, thought-provoking book develops the thesis that theology must think in terms of spaces as science did some decades ago. He speaks of a supra-polar space which transcends the world-form of polarity, not by annihilating the entire contents of this form, but by recasting it. This space is not the full reality of God but a side which is turned to us. It is the archetypal space of eternity in which man and God really meet in the I-Thou relationship. Faith then is faith, not in the God of a two-story universe, but in God whose reality is revealed in the super-polar space which encompasses all reality.[8]

Such thinking honors the respective areas of science and religion, but also attempts to combine the essential givens of each. The success of such efforts will depend on more than mental acumen. In the last analysis it will hinge on man's acceptance of that City which embraces all truth, goodness, and beauty.

Evolution

It would relieve tensions and avoid misunderstanding if the conflict between science and religion were lifted to the level of dialogue in which the protagonists would be wiser than antagonists. The bloodless warfare would then become a sincere searching for truth that requires calmness rather than confusion.

Great harm is done when the scientist succumbs to a scientism not warranted by the facts, nor even permitted by the strict procedures of the natural sciences. Equally great harm is done when the Christian remains unmoved by the evidence disclosed by the sciences. It is foolish to quarrel with facts, to be insensitive to the growth of knowledge.

Knowledge, however, implies more than the factual. Interpretation is essential; and it is here that the clash occurs. Basically there is no disagreement between science and the Christian faith. The difference arises from the view of life and the world with which one begins and continues. The mechanist and the naturalist theorizing on the facts of science exclude the supernatural. The Christian recognizes the supernatural as well as the natural, stressing the response of the whole man to a two-fold revelation.

Are the givens of the sciences and "the scientific outlook" sufficient to satisfy the quest for meaning? Have the humanities little value? Can the concern of religion be dismissed because scientism is in the saddle and logical positivism busies itself largely with referrents?

Anthony Standen, himself a scientist, has some caustic things to say about the sophistry which overextends the scientific method into areas where it does not belong. He asks if there were no intelligent men before science was born. He warns against the dreadful cocksureness of those who violate the true spirit of science. It is his conviction that the first purpose of science is to learn about God and to admire Him through His handiwork.[9]

The theory of evolution, based on the methods and findings of science, has brought light to some, confusion to many, and the challenge to come to a greater understanding to us all. The Christian reaction should be, not in terms of diatribe, but in terms of dialogue that seeks for clarity without the surrender of those convictions molded by the light of divine revelation.

It is heartening to know that Christian men of scientific, philosophical, and theological competence are meeting the problem with a freshness that bolsters the assurance of the intelligent believer.

The shock caused by Darwin's *Origin of Species* and *Descent of Man,* Huxley's popularizing, Haeckel's conclusions, and Spencer's philosophy is not as great as it was in the nineteenth century. Since that time scientific knowledge has grown from more to more. The Christian thinker, honoring facts and truth wherever he finds them, is concerned primarily with proving or disproving in the area of interpretation.

Anthony Standen maintains that there is an overwhelming mass of evidence to prove the vague theory of evolution, but also insists that the precise theory has never been proved.[10]

It is, therefore, in the area of interpretation that the theory must be examined. The mass of evidence gathered from several sciences is there for the undaunted mind. No one can be an expert in all the fields; and therefore there must be a mutual trust. But knowledge must honor the expert in other fields besides those of the descriptive sciences. This is where the dialogue takes on significance.

At this point we recall what G. T. W. Patrick offered as a twentieth-century caution years ago. He said that though the story of science is a true story, it is not the whole story and perhaps not the most interesting part.[11]

The Christian thinker, dealing with evolution, also stresses a very important part of the story. He is opposed to the doctrine or dogma of naturalistic evolution but not to the idea of development understood in God's creative activity.

Decades ago Bavinck insisted that the doctrine of creation and the idea of development are not necessarily contradictory. The creation of heaven and earth recorded in Genesis 1:1 preceded the work of the six days of creation related in Genesis 1:33 ff. The six days of creation need not necessarily be considered days of twenty-four hours. The first three days may have been unusual, cosmic days, and even the last three may have shared in this characteristic.[12]

The irenic theologian, however, rejects the theory of man's

descent from the animal. Scripture teaches plainly that man, physically and psychically, was created fullgrown — in the image of God — with consciousness and freedom.[13]

Other Christian thinkers, specialists in their own field, hold to the doctrine of creation. That God created the world and man is a conviction. How it all happened is another matter. Scripture in simple narrative is emphatic about creation including that of man. Science knows nothing about origins. Zoology, paleontology, genetics, geology, and the related sciences can throw much light on the *how*, and for that we are grateful. Such knowledge should guard us against naive and benighted points of view for which unenlightened man, not the Word of God, is responsible.

Jan Lever, the brilliant zoologist of the Free University of Amsterdam, a confirmed Christian of the Calvinistic stamp, has contributed a scholarly work to an understanding of the problem.[14] He is a creationist convinced that evolution contributes much to an understanding of the *how* of creation. Man may be the end-result of a developmental process, but he is nevertheless that special creature made in the image of God with the powers of reason, emotions, and will, and the gift of faith. His distinctiveness differentiates him from a universe millions of years old and from all other animate creatures.

Mention must also be made of an excellent symposium by thirteen Christian scientists and theologians who assess the theory of evolution, and re-examine the scriptural data bearing on origin and organic development.[15] Here is an openmindedness to scientific facts and the interpretations based on these, and also a profound loyalty to the Word of God which inspires the Christian faith. A careful reading of this book should open eyes and minds to the difficult problems involved but also to the fact that the Christian faith at its best is not obscurantist.

In past centuries the Church has lost some battles with science. It should not go on repeating the defeats. On the contrary it can and does win where and when it emphasizes the distinctiveness of man as revealed in God's revelation. Even if it should be proved that there was a transition from the prehuman to the human stage, there is still enough of mystery and of miracle in man's being a person for whom Jesus Christ died. When Thomas Carlyle in the presence of scholars discussed the descent of man and was asked to give his view, he replied, "Gentlemen, you place man a little higher than a tadpole. I hold with the ancient psalmist (Psalm 8): 'Thou hast made him a little lower than the angels.' "

The question of origins is a significant one, but the fact of redemption is still more important. A knowledge of origins is small comfort without the certainty about destiny and destination. The theory of evolution has no unqualified answer as to man's origin and destiny. Nineteenth-century optimism has been more than dampened by the course of events. Twentieth-century pessimism and the more recent assertion on the part of some that man has come of age still leave man on the stage with no assurance that progressive stages will fulfill whatever promises he cherishes.

It is the Christian's task and privilege to be scholarly, or at least to appreciate all knowledge. But by divine grace he also has the illumination of faith, a higher knowledge, a positive trust in Him who alone can guide man's steps aright from origins to destiny. The Christian faith is indispensable in this post-Christian age, though the Christian, like the martyrs, may be expendable.

NOTES

1. Warren C. Young, *A Christian Approach to Philosophy* (Wheaton: Van Kampen Press, 1954), p. 80.
2. Herman Bavinck, *Gereformeerde Dogmatiek* (Kampen: J. H. Kok, 1906), I, p. 388.
3. Herman Bavinck, *Christelijke Wetenschap* (Kampen: J. H. Kok, 1904), p. 44.
4. John Baillie, *Natural Science and the Spiritual Life* (New York: Oxford, 1951), p. 25.
5. *Ibid.*, p. 31.

6. See also John Baillie's *What is Christian Civilization?* (New York: Scribners, 1945).

7. H. H. Price, *Some Aspects of the Conflict Between Science and Religion* (New York: Cambridge University Press, 1953), p. 28.

8. Karl Heim, *Christian Faith and Natural Science* (New York: Harper Torchbooks, 1957).

9. Anthony Standen, *Science is a Sacred Cow* (New York: Dutton, 1950), p. 200.

10. *Ibid.,* p. 103.

11. G. T. W. Patrick, *Introduction to Philosophy* (Boston: Houghton Mifflin, 1924), p. 152.

12. Herman Bavinck, *Gereformeerde Dogmatiek* (Kampen: J. H. Kok, 1908), II, pp. 529, 533.

13. *Ibid.,* p. 573

14. See Jan Lever's *Creation and Evolution,* trans. by Dr. Peter G. Berkhout, (Grand Rapids: Grand Rapids International Publications, 1958).

15. Anderson, V. Elving, and others, *Evolution and Christian Thought Today,* Russel L. Mixter, ed. (Grand Rapids: Eerdmans, 1959).

IX

Science and the Humanities

Though science is not the invention of the twentieth century, it has made greater strides in the last decade than in the long years of scientific endeavor that went before.

Besides the cleavage and conflict between science and religion there is another rift, that between science and the humanities. The acceleration in scientific knowledge brings the problem home to us more than ever before.

It needs no long memory to grasp what the progress of Russian experiments in space did to our American inertia and pride. Education, somewhat panic-stricken, bolted more than ever in the direction of the sciences. Stimulated by Government's concern and investment, the marathon to Mars and the moon is on. The accomplishments are beyond our wildest dreams, if one may still speak of dreams in our science-conditioned age.

Fortunately, education, which in this country had been drifting farther away from the humanities, has veered somewhat into a saner course. Educators, government, and industry have sensed what the loss of a liberal arts program would mean. There is an awareness that specialization readily breeds ignorance and divisiveness, both of which are destructive of human wholeness.

The rift, or better, the debate, between science and the humanities is of long standing. It was inevitable when men like Francis Bacon, Copernicus, and Galileo challenged medieval concern and emphases. They did not desire to dump the humanities, the classics. There was, however, in them the urgency to study nature and the universe at first hand with their eye on the object. The telescope, the microscope, the test tube, and all the intricate instruments of the laboratory have enriched man's knowledge and understanding.

It was in the nineteenth century that the claims of science were advanced by Herbert Spencer and Thomas Huxley, and the claims of the humanities by Matthew Arnold.

Spencer's *Education,* appearing two years after the publication of Darwin's *Origin of Species,* stressed the importance of science. His educational theories grew out of his conception of man as an animal and his ideas about adaptation to environment. For him the best education is that which prepares for direct and indirect self-preservation, for parenthood, for citizenship, and for the "miscellaneous refinements of life." In other words Spencer brought the humanities in last with an indulging shrug, speaking of them as the "haughty sisters" who "flaunt their fripperies in the eyes of the world."

Huxley, the popularizer of Darwin, insisted that training in the natural sciences should be the main part of education at least for the great majority of mankind. He spoke, perhaps with playful sarcasm, of "the Levites of culture" and of "the caterwauling of poets."

It was Matthew Arnold who took up the rapier, rather than the cudgels, against what he considered the overemphasis on science. He had a strong appreciation for the humanities and even for science, provided the latter did not become the dog in the manger. In this regard his views had more in common with Huxley than with Spencer. Arnold, the apostle of culture, not of the "kid-glove" persuasion as some diatribes would have it, presented his thoughts clearly in *Essays in Criticism* and in *Culture and Anarchy.* But it is especially in his lecture on "Literature and Science," delivered in America in 1883, that he addressed himself to the problem of how far literature and the natural sciences can walk together and where they must part.

Arnold, concerned about the sense in us for conduct and the sense in us for beauty, stresses the importance of the humanities in education. Admitting that there is much in Plato that is obsolete, he quotes with approval the philosopher's words: "An intelligent man will prize these studies which result in his soul getting soberness, righteousness, and wisdom, and will less value the others." Such training is valuable whether it prepares a person "for an hereditary seat in the House of Lords or for the pork trade in Chicago."

This is not said with condescension as if the great results of scientific studies deserve only a secondary place. He agrees with Huxley that they are a part of our culture, though they should not be made the staple of our education. Moreover, he corrects the mistaken notion held by those scientists who think of the humanities as more or less of Greek and Roman *belles lettres*. For Arnold the glory of Greece and Rome lay in their history, art, poetry, and eloquence. In these lies the power of refreshing and delighting us, and even the power of helping us to relate the results of modern science to our need for moral conduct and our need for beauty.

In *Culture and Anarchy* Arnold defines culture as "a pursuit of our total perfection by means of getting to know, on all matters which most concern us, the best which has been thought and said in the world." This should call forth the response of the whole man constantly faced by the challenge of old and new knowledge and the claims of high morality.

It is understandable that the debate between science and the humanities has carried over into our century and is very much alive today. C. P. Snow in *The Two Cultures* maintains that there is no communication between literary people and scientific men, that there is indifference and even at times hostility. This polarization he sees as sheer loss. There is both humor and seriousness in his anecdote about a group of Oxford men gathered at mealtime. An older man, a humanist, is talking radiantly about his subject, but the other men look at him as if to say, "What's he talking about?" The Vice-chancellor attempts to come to the rescue by singling out one of the men and saying, "Don't mind him. He's a mathematician. We don't talk to him."

Snow, a literary man as well as scientist, goes on to a praising of the scientific revolution which in its technological aspect has contributed immensely to the enriching of the have-nots as well as the haves. He even jibes at those "pure" scientists who in their ivory laboratories sneer at technology.

Perhaps we can arrive at a better understanding of our problem by considering three forces that have come to plague us: specialization, mechanization, and massification. It is understandable that they have appeared; it is inexcusable that they should dominate man.

Specialization

The astounding and at times terrifying advance in scientific knowledge has brought about an atomization that defies the sense of wholeness. Scientists, each engaged in his field or fraction thereof, can no longer communicate. It is true that there is some interrelatedness or we could not send men into space. But specialization is on the increase for the simple reason that no man can know everything. For that reason it is of primary importance that scientists become more than specialists, that they strive to be whole men concerned about understanding as well as specific information.

Even in the humanities specialization with its accompanying professionalism has taken its toll. A specialist, engaged in tracking punctuation from Beowulf to Thomas Wolfe, or a scholar immersed in tracking down some obscure writer in the seventeenth century may speak with questionable modesty of their ignorance about Homer and Milton. So the atomization runs on as the cave supplants the mountain peak.

What is of serious concern is the widening gulf between science and the humanities. When men speak today of knowledge explosion, they usually imply the vast accumulation of scientific knowledge which is changing our civilization from hour to hour. In this emphasis on the sciences there lies the danger. Eric Weil says, "What has happened is that modern science has become autonomous, a value in itself."[1] And Loren Eisely writes, "Our investment in man, it has been justly remarked, is deteriorating even as the financial investment in science grows."[2]

At this point we might well say with Cassius:

> The fault, dear Brutus, is not in our stars,
> But in ourselves, that we are underlings.

Man suffers much from narrow horizons or from none at all, from exclusion more than from inclusion. Can one imagine a convention of physicists listening to Sara Teasdale's quest for beauty, or a group of bank directors relishing a review of Mary Webb's *Precious Bane,* or a seaman's union studying "The Ancient Mariner"?

Yet an individual physicist, or banker, or seaman might well be reading these works of art and insight which go far beyond any specialization. For they are human, and as such is there anything human that should be foreign to them?

In that direction lies the exit from too much specialization. Science as well as the humanities demands imagination. A scientist cannot specialize without something of the sense of wonder in his field. His field widens whenever he embraces his wife and children as more than formulae or equations. An astronaut or cosmonaut, alert to everything in his capsule, still exclaims about the beauty of the earth, and even a flash of Homer may pass through his mind like lightning.

Under the impact of logical positivism and the scientific method, philosophy today has become analytical. It is engaged in linguistics, the meaning of terms. That has significance, but unfortunately this quest for meaning fails to take into consideration the wholeness of man, who he is, why he is here, and where he is going. The Greek mind at its best was interested in consistent thinking with an eye to understanding.

Christian thinkers have had and still have that basic concern. Man, if he is to be truly that, must explore, not only the atom, or the distant stars, or words, but also the mind and the heart.

Mechanization

Science and its offspring, technology, have immersed us in the machine age more and more. This has its advantages in making us feel more comfortable, but the comforts have not presented man with the ultimate comfort in life and in death. The IBM machine, all the experiments in laboratories and in space, the surfeit of a stainless steel paradise have not dispelled the anxiety of our age. They cannot clarify man's spiritual and moral problems; they do not answer to man's invincible surmise. Mary Shelley's *Frankenstein* is still a directive we cannot blink away.

As man did not shake off his problems by entering a monastery, so he does not rid himself of his moral obligations by conquering space. His feet may find rest in the dust of the moon, but his heart will still cry for solutions that have evaded him on earth.

Massification

It would be unfair to blame science and its cumulative impact entirely for this affliction. Other forces have contributed, as is evident from Kierkegaard's tirade against massification in the nineteenth century. But experimentation and invention have brought on a standardization against which even the "pure" scientist may rebel. Man has become the beneficiary of gadgets and at the same time their victim to the point that he is unaware of the plague of conformity. Advertising is doing its share, stimulating desires rather than emphasizing human needs. It all seems to make for economic prosperity but also for a loss as to what is specifically human.

Totalitarianism thrives in a machine age and can whip the

masses into subjection and conformity with the promise of a kingdom of things. Under such conditions the payoff easily becomes more and more of less and less. Governmental paternalism, envisioning a technological millennium, produces more conformists than Thoreaus escaping to Walden Pond.

What then is the answer? Several years ago Douglas Bush wrote: "Since divinity is gone and philosophy has abandoned its concern for the good life, it is through literature that we get an understanding of man's moral and religious quest."[3] Literature is a reflection on, and a criticism of, life. It may analyze man and put him together again within the framework of eternal verities, or it may fragmentize him, revealing the tragic loss when human wholeness becomes a mirage. At its best, however, its aim is to humanize man and society. Its concern is with the entire range and richness of life and the individual's response to these. Sophocles, Dante, Shakespeare, and Milton never split the atom, but they did crack the heart, mind, and conscience of man, disclosing even to us what made him tick or stop ticking. In all great literature there sounds the warning that without vision a people perish.

The humanities keep alive that perennial concern about the meaningful. That requires faith and vision with a strong dash of the imagination. It seems impossible to study flora and fauna, the specimens of geology and archaeology, and even the givens of the laboratories without conjuring up great images that lie behind them. Even as history is more than a recounting of dry-as-dust facts, as is evident from Arnold Toynbee and Will Durant, so science implies more than the methodical and factual. It is a great jump from Darwin to Teilhard de Chardin who combines religious and mystical vision with scientific perceptiveness. Evolution may be affirmed or denied, but it cannot be dealt with as trivial when it envisions the past and man's destiny and destination.

Perhaps a word of appreciation is in order for those naturalists who may not be in the books of the "pure" scientists. We think of men like John Burroughs, Ernest Thompson

Seton, and William Beebe who introduced the nonspecialists to the mysteries of nature. We recall Jules Verne who in some ways saw the possibility of the impossible. Our present day writers of science fiction have their work cut out for them.

In the debate between science and the humanities it is to be hoped that wholeness will win over atomization. Both must join forces against ignorance and despair. There is room for greater conquests. The conquest lies in the realm of man but more tellingly in that area where man meets the eternal. Gazing at the pyramids or the Parthenon, reflecting on a primrose by the river's brink or the flower in the crannied wall, being more than a spectator at Browning's "The Grammarian's Funeral," thinking with Plato, or soaring with Milton — what are these but accent on the mystery that calls for the human adventure. And contemplating the Cross, where for the Christian all roads meet, will clarify where man and gadgets fail.

Whoever wrote it was right when he said:

> Here lies the man of magic,
> Deep beneath the sod.
> He got his every gadget,
> But forgot his God.

NOTES

1. Eric Weil, "Science and Modern Culture," *Daedalus,* (Winter, 1965).
2. Loren Eisely, "The Illusion of the Two Cultures," *The American Scholar,* (Summer, 1964).
3. Douglas Bush, "Education and the Humanities," *Daedalus,* (Winter, 1959).

X

The Christian Approach to Beauty

Is there a normal person whose soul is so dead that the sense of wonder is completely lost? Wordsworth seemed to think so when he presented Peter Bell to whom a primrose by the river's brink was only a primrose, and nothing more. Yet, most of us have human reactions whether we are gazing at Mt. Evans from the valley or at Mont Blanc from an airplane, or standing on a peak in Darien to watch the Pacific for the first time, or poetizing at sunset in the Bad Lands, or listening with soul-tugging emotions to an oratorio, or bending over the rhododendron on the hillsides, or sitting rigid under the spell of *Macbeth,* or watching the cactus wren feed her young.

All these experiences may not come to one person; nor may any of them come with equal force to everyone. There is, however, the sense of wonder, God's gift to man, to lift him, at least for a spell, from the daily ruts. Under an overarching sky, full of sunshine and occasional clouds by day, and full of stars and a changing moon by night, man's imagination must fly upward.

It is one thing to have some or all of these experiences; it is quite another to theorize about them. Our aesthetic reactions usually go beyond the telling. The scientist may pick the rainbow apart and slice the wings of the lunar moth, but he must also acknowledge the mystery that remains.

There is something satisfying about the pursuit of the factual and the actual. There is also something noble in the confession that beauty and our experience of it lie beyond the laboratory

94

and the blue-print. The ignoble lies in the sluggish satisfaction with facts and with vague feelings, with no desire to penetrate the mystery.

The nature of our subject demands that we as Christians come to grips with beauty and with it experiencing, and with art as the crystalization of beauty. That there are hurdles in the path of our discussion we cannot deny. Therefore, we must go forward with care.

An Unpopular Subject?

Christians who take the Word and the Reformation emphasis seriously are very much concerned about salvation and the whole plan of God bringing that about. Along with that concern there goes a theological-mindedness, a desire to think through the Bible and its application to life.

This is commendable. There is always the danger, however, of an impoverishing exclusiveness. Accepting the Bible as God's revelation of truth, we may ignore it as the divine revelation of beauty. Dr. B. Wielenga had this in mind when he wrote: "We also know that in our Christian Netherlands, because of suspicion and shortsightedness, many have despised art and the life of beauty in general because they were so blind to the exemplary beauty of the Bible, because they were ignorant and without feeling in regard to art as the gift of God."[1] Bavinck makes a similar criticism in his essay, *"Van Schoonheid and Schoonheidsleer"* (Of Beauty and Aesthetics) when he mildly charges his people with a certain rudeness and stiffness in regard to beauty and art, and ends by saying that "next to truth and goodness, beauty also deserves our homage."[2]

Besides being very religious and theological the Christian has a strong sense of duty, that "stern Daughter of the Voice of God." Seeing life under the aspect of eternity, he takes it seriously. There are his personal relations to God, to family and home, to his fellowmen, to business, to his job, to the

Church and to the Kingdom. Busy at being God's creature in these varied fields, what time does he have for beauty and for art? He may appreciate these or perhaps tolerate them as so much frippery and ornamentation, of interest only to pagan and frivolous souls. There may be a carved ivory elephant on the coffee table, hymns on records, a plaque on the wall, and a well-designed car in the garage, but his prime passion is still utility wedded to duty.

We Christians can easily succumb to a benevolent materialism, not spurning a mountain side nor a prairie vista, but keeping our desires near the refrigerator and the oven and our eyes on the ticker tape. We know that, like Abraham, we look for a city, yet the pins of our dwellings must be secure; and securities must not escape us. Our Lord has taught us to pray for as much bread as we need daily, but if we extend that a little, what is the harm?

The statement has been made by Christians that strength lies in isolation. One must, however, be careful of misapplication. There is something magnificent about the world and life view of Calvinism which takes in the whole realm of nature and of grace. But the denial of it or a fractional application may result in more backyard then vista. In the area of beauty and art this can be very damaging.

The Christian may and must practice informed selectivity when it comes to the aesthetic; but grave danger lies in excluding too much that is essential. Westcott in his essay on "The Relation of Christianity to Art" reminds us of the statement made at the Council of Nicea: "The making of pictures is not the invention of artists but the admitted legislation and tradition of the Catholic Church."[3] He adds that this view was, of course, fatal to art. In spite of the depth and broadness of our view in theory, we can impoverish ourselves in practice.

With all our genuine concern for the Christian life, our serious sense of duty, our puritan industriousness, and our fear of worldliness, is there any room left for the contemplation of beauty, the cultivation of the aesthetic sense, and the creativity that art demands? Is there any hunger and thirst for theory and practice, for understanding, and for actual accomplishment in this field?

There must be and there is. We have said that the subject is not popular, at least not in the sense that our personal religion and our gaining a livelihood are popular. We may not have cared to think deeply about it because of other interests. Yet, who is there among us that has not been moved inwardly by some aspect of nature, a psalm, some creative act of an artist in poem, music, color, or stone? There are those who have gone beyond these primary reactions, who like Abt Vogler have framed "out of three sounds, not a fourth sound, but a star."

Whether our aesthetic sense is in its infancy or more mature, we Christians have an obligation to think about it and to look for the roots of the experience.

A First Duty Concerning Beauty

We have chosen the word *duty* purposely because that must appeal to our Christian seriousness and sincerity. Religiously and morally we know where our obligations lie. Thinking of beauty in terms of duty will round out our lives all the more.

Our first duty is to recognize God as the source from whom truth, goodness, and beauty spring. The Word, God's revelation of Himself, is filled with the concept of the divine glory.

It is an education in itself to look up in a concordance the many places in the Scriptures where this concept appears. We suggest only a few of these. The glory of God appeared to Moses in the burning thorn bush and later in the pillar of fire and on Mount Sinai where the Law was given. It was evident in the Holy of Holies in the Temple. Reference to it is made time and again in the Psalms. Think of Psalm 19: "The heavens declare the glory of God." Isaiah beheld it in his vision in the Temple. At the birth of Jesus the glory of the Lord shone round about the shepherds. Speaking of Jesus' coming John says, ". . . we beheld his glory . . . full of grace and truth." The manifestation appears again on the Mount of Transfiguration. Paul on the Damascus road was blinded by it. Jesus is called "the Lord of Glory." And the doxologies of the saints in heaven and on earth constantly echo the song of the angels in Ephrata's meadows: "Glory to God in the highest."

Though we cannot go into a thorough search of this concept here, a study of Scripture certainly warrants our saying that the divine glory implies that wonderful manifestation of God's attributes which is always a revealing in beauty and therefore a revelation of beauty from its very source.

Glory means dazzling light, radiance, but also revelation. That glory which blinded some and caused others to cover their faces comes to us also with less than blinding force. It is not God's purpose to blind us but to open our eyes and to sharpen our senses. That is exactly what revelation is for. Because God has made Himself known, we can apprehend something of His glory in which beauty is a factor. In creation and redemption we are alerted to stupendous events in which the beauty of the Lord our God leaps into flame. When eternity not only overarches time but enters it, the glories of the everlasting must illumine the temporal scene and point man beyond the ruts where time must have a stop.

In the beginning creation was infused with the divine beauty. The vestiges remain with us today in spite of the imperfections. When God saw all that He had made, He declared it good. As Wielenga reminds us, the Hebrew word used is the very one that describes Queen Esther as beautiful or lovely. The implication is that the good and the beautiful are very closely related.

Reflections on the creation are expressed in the highest poetic form as is evident from such Psalms as the 19th and the 104th. Those passages which tell of the coming Christian era and of the new creation are among the finest in literature. Excellent examples are chapters 11, 35, 40, and 55 of Isaiah.

Descriptions of our final destiny and of the Holy City in the closing chapters of Revelation are an invitation to glory. The wheel comes full circle, for man's beginnings in Eden culminate in the New Jerusalem far outshining the pale dream of man's utopias. If the apocalyptic impact is almost too much for man's imagination, it is not quite so; for he was made for such a destiny.

The glory of God is evident also in the revelation and the actualizing of redemption. Here under God man comes into his own again. For sin is ugly. It has made man ugly, and it has dulled and darkened his senses, also the feeling for beauty. But because of the divine grace sin destroyed neither man, nor beauty, nor the aesthetic sense.

Beauty also comes into its own again in Jesus Christ. He is the restorer of all things and of man. He is the Light of the world, and we have seen His glory. It is true that as the Suffering Servant in Isaiah 53 He has no form or comeliness, and we hid our faces from Him. That was what our guilt and sin have done to Him. It is in the Cross and the Resurrection that truth, goodness, and beauty triumph, and we become beneficiaries through grace. Of course we know that it is not the beauty of Jesus that saves us, but neither are we redeemed without it. There is a spiritual and moral beauty about our Lord that should be reflected in us. The sun is beneficial for man, animals, and plants. They all need the light and the heat, but they cannot cast the glory aside. So the rays of the Sun of Righteousness penetrate us and are reflected again in order that by the divine power and grace we rise to our destined stature.

God, who is the highest Truth, Goodness, and Beauty, has allowed these to flood creation. Abraham Kuyper puts it uniquely when he speaks of "God's playing with his Spirit in the world." Beauty, which is of spiritual and supernatural origin and character, is part of man's inheritance. By virtue of creation man also has the aesthetic sense, not as ornamentation, but as bound up with truth and goodness.

In Ecclesiastes 3:11 we read that God "has made everything beautiful in its time" as well as "put eternity into man's
mind." The glory which flows from the divine wisdom, and
truth, and goodness is ours for the asking. It is there whether
we see it or not. It is evident from Genesis through Revelation,
in creation, in history, and in ultimate renewal. Like Abraham
we look for the city in which the divine glory shall be clearly
made known.

It is true that the serious and sincere Christian is concerned
with that saving grace which alone restores man. That is
Biblical. Both Old and New Testaments stress the history of
redemption and the personal experience of salvation. Let it
be said honestly, frankly, and unashamedly that we Christians
are concerned about this vital matter; but it is essential to
add that our redemption is bound up with the restoration of all
things. It is the glory of God that takes seriously the glory of
restored man and creation. As Phillips has it in his version
of Romans 8:19, the whole creation is standing on tiptoe
waiting with eager longing for the revealing of the sons of God.

Art As Privilege and Responsibility

Art is not a mere copying of nature. A painting is not a
photograph. Art is the creative expression of beauty by a
gifted person in whatever medium he is working. It requires
feeling, perception, appreciation, imagination, and a God-given
skill not common to everyone. Browning's Abt Vogler says:

> But God has a few of us whom he whispers
>   in the ear;
> The rest may reason and welcome: 'tis we
>   musicians know.

The artist has innate gifts and the urge to cultivate them.
That way he can become a seer and a knower to delight and
instruct us.

God has not limited the aesthetic sense and creative ability to those who are twice-born. In fact the arts have flourished more outside the circle of God's people than within. The Almighty uses His agents where and how He wills; and the Christian must learn to enjoy the divine gifts also in the lives of the unreconciled. We recall that Cain and his descendants founded cities and contributed to the spread of civilization, and that Hiram built the Temple. In his *Institutes* Calvin reminds us of "how many gifts the Lord has left in possession of human nature," and warns us that "in despising the gifts, we insult the Giver."[4] In his lecture on "Calvinism and Art'" Kuyper refers to the glory that was and is Greece, speaking of the "election of the Greeks for the revelation of art."[5] He insists that Calvinism aided in emancipating art from the Church and that its stress on the simple life, the commonplace, made its impact on the development of painting as is evident from the canvases of Rembrandt. It also encouraged creativity in literature and music.

If it is an ordinary statement, it is still a thought-provoking one, that religion and art have been most closely related. A reading of the Greek tragedies, a breath-taking view of the Parthenon, a study of the mystery religions, an appreciation of the architecture of European cathedrals and churches and of the paintings, mosaics, and tapestries treasured in them, a knowledge of the best in literature and music throughout the Christian era up to the present day — all this and more is evidence enough.

Styles in the varied arts have come and gone, but the best has lasted to make up the heritage of the ages. If, as Santayana said, "Art is a delayed echo," it gives expression to what men believe, and think, and feel, or to what they have ceased to believe, and think, and feel.

The fact that all art is not religious should not disturb us anymore than the fact that economics, politics, and the sciences are not religious. A healthy Christian outlook recognizes a certain sovereignty inherent in each sphere, a sovereignty that is not to be intimidated by external pressures.

This is not saying that religion and morals have nothing to contribute to these spheres. For man is a whole being whose wholeness demands his living in, and responding to, many spheres on which religion and morals make a definite impact.

In the past much has been said about "art for art's sake." If this means that art has a certain independence with rules of its own not to be dictated to by a cold rationalism, or bourgeois mediocrity, or ignorant prudishness, well and good. Pegasus cannot rise with clipped wings. If art demands complete autonomy, however, it severs its relationship with truth and goodness. That way it becomes fractional in communication and often meaningless.

A visit to the Guggenheim Museum in New York or a surveying of the sculpture dotting the walks and lawns around the Shakespeare Theater in Stratford, Ontario, may be more baffling than revealing. If art is expression, that should imply communication. Is it enough that the artist has satisfied himself, or that he consoles the spectator by telling him to read into or out of his work whatever he pleases? Or is the "delayed echo" only an expression of the meaninglessness of existence in a post-Christian era?

Perhaps in painting, sculpture, and music we should not expect the clarity we find in the written word. That would demand a getting inside the artist. Yet, the greater artist and the greater art have a way of getting inside us. That may be the telling quality.

The written word may also be baffling, as for example in some of our contemporary poetry and the theater of the absurd. Here too we must honor new skills and techniques that defy the accustomed manner. Old prejudices and the approach with the top of our minds should give way to imagination and feeling that are essential to grasping the intangible. But the fact and the challenge are still there that the poet and dramatist should be concerned about communication which is more than monologue.

Art has been with us a long time for the enrichment of life.

If Christianity has its "cultured despisers," it will not do for the Christian to return the compliment. Art at its best deals with beauty in relation to truth and goodness, at times even by indirection, by contrast, by presenting the ugly. It traffics in the real and the ideal. When it forfeits the ideal, it still portrays the loss. Much of our contemporary literature, for example, assumes that God is dead, but it thrives on borrowed capital, implying by indirection the grandeur that man has squandered for the misery against which he protests.

The intelligent Christian appreciates art as the gift of God's grace. He enjoys beauty wherever he finds it, not as ornamentation, nor as a substitute for faith. It is his privilege and responsibility to cultivate the arts as a reflection of the divine glory.

NOTES

1. B. Wielenga, *De Bijbel Als Boek Van Schoonheid* (Kampen: J. H. Kok, 1925), p. 14.
2. Herman Bavinck, *Verzamelde Opstellen* (Kampen: J. H. Kok, 1921), p. 200.
3. Brook F. Westcott, *Epistles of St. John* (Grand Rapids: Eerdmans, 1950), p. 355.
4. John Calvin, *Institutes* (Edinburgh: Clark), I, p. 236.
5. Abraham Kuyper, *Calvinism*, the Stone Lectures (Höneker and Wormser, 1908), p. 218

XI

The Christian Faith and Secularism

Men of insight — prophets, poets, novelists, dramatists, philosophers — and the Word of God have spoken to this subject.

Christopher Morley in that delightful book, *Where the Blue Begins,* has one of his characters say, "Modern skepticism has amputated God from the heart, but there is still a twinge where the arteries were sewn up." And again, "The churches were so hemmed in by tall buildings they had no chance to kneel." We easily call to mind Trinity Church at the foot of Wall Street in New York, dwarfed by towering skyscrapers.

We recall the words of T. S. Eliot about what happens where the Word is not spoken. The encroaching desert takes its toll, and the desert is in the heart of man.

Jesus, our Lord, understanding life in all its segments and in all its unity, has left us such imperishable warnings as these:

> A man's life consists not in the abundance of things he possesses.
>
> You are more than many sparrows.
>
> Lay not up for yourselves treasures on earth. . . . but lay up for yourselves treasures in heaven.

These quotations and many more point to the baffling yet challenging problems that perplex and console the serious mind.

The Importance of the Secular

We must make a distinction between the secular and secularism. These terms have their origin in the word *saeculum,* meaning *age* or *world.*

In our criticism of secularism it is our task to appreciate the secular. We must not drain the baby away with the waters of the bath.

God is the Creator-God, not Aristotle's Prime Mover, not Thought thinking upon thought with no concern for the world and man.

In Psalm 24 we read: "The earth is the Lord's and the fulness thereof, the world and those who dwell therein." (Interestingly enough these words are inscribed above the Bank of England.)

Our Creator called the universe into existence, not in time, but with time as Augustine says. He made a God's-plenty of matter. Man has known this for a long time, but it is impressed on him more and more in this age of stellar adventure and space exploration. When God created man in His own image, He placed him on this earth with the stars as a canopy. As part of the divine image man also received lordship over creation with no restrictions except the warning against pride which could cause the tragic fall of angels and of men. In spite of the fall the world is still the theater of God's glory, as Calvin says.

Our God created man as the bearer of the divine image. As far as we know man is the only soul and body creature who can believe, think, feel, and will, and who by grace can utilize the implications of his lordship.

As we have seen in Chapter III the God of the Christian is a revealing God. There are two revelations requiring the sensitivity of faith as response.

It is especially from the Scriptures that we receive the proper perspective on man and the world and therefore also on the secular. It clarifies beyond the best efforts of a natural theology.

Secularism

Secularism has been defined or described in various ways. It has been called the refusal to let God be God, and it has been characterized as practical atheism. If it does not in every case deny religion, it does express the denial of its relevance to the major areas of life. Secularism concerns itself with dominating interests other than loyalty to God.

Words from Deuteronomy 32:15 throw a clear light on this perennial problem. "But Jeshurun waxed fat and kicked; you waxed fat, you grew thick, you became sleek; then he forsook God who made him, and scoffed at the Rock of his salvation." In other words, Israel, lightly esteeming God, had turned to secularism.

Though this apostasy is as old as sin, it is referred to in modern times as rooted in the Renaissance. The thrust of that glorious and at times inglorious movement has been summed up in Swinburne's familiar words: "Glory to Man in the highest, for Man is the Master of things."

Shailer Matthews once used the phrase: "God emeritus." This shocking phrase, which still leaves God alive, is no figment of the imagination but a candid description of a tragic severance that leaves man scarcely suffering a twinge.

The shift to nature, the present-day emphasis on science are certainly not to be despised. But preoccupation with the horizontal has contributed to the atrophying of the sense of mystery, the ineffable, the holy. As Samuel Miller says, "Everything has become natural, biological, social, and quite clinical."[1] The universe and man with all his skills are very much in the picture, but God is not. On the death of John Burroughs, a friend of the naturalist said, "Poor John, he knew the garden; he never met the Gardener."

In *Christian Faith and Natural Science* Karl Heim speaks of two kinds of secularists. There are those who keep fighting God, and there are those mature secularists who are perfectly adjusted to a godless situation. He illustrates from a novel entitled *The Jeromin Children*. In this story the great-grandfather fulminates against the God for whom he has only contempt, but the great-grandson has become a serene secularist completely adjusted to the natural world without any intimations of transcendence.

We have with us and have had for some time the religious atheists who are not devoid of fervor. Marx, Feuerbach, and Freud have their disciples. We think also of the gloomy existentialists marooned in their cellophane wrappers, filled with anxiety about death, staring at Nothingness, yet drumming up courage to face the absurd.

The Fruits of Secularization

The bitter fruits are no concern of the mature secularist, though they still seem to bother his fellow travelers who are less serene. They are, however, of greatest concern to the Christian.

One of the results of secularism is dehumanization. It is a strong term, but it reaches the heart of the matter. Very likely Gabriel Marcel had it in mind when he said, "Man has become a function." It implies that there is no profound maturing of mind and heart. Science, the machine, organization, and massification have pushed man from the center of things. It spells spiritual tragedy, a return to chaos and the jungle.

We are reminded of Sören Kierkegaard's lone battle, in the nineteenth century, against "the system" in church and society, against massification with its herd mentality, and his pleading with "that solitary individual" to be the man God wants him to be.

Secularism results in fragmentation, pluralism, a loss of unity. In our time we have with a vengeance separation of church and state, of religion from education, of meaning from art. Philosophy has become the concern for the logic of words. According to Matthew Arnold there is no seeing of life steadily and wholly as Sophocles saw it. To speak of our age as pagan may be insulting to those Greeks who had a richer conception of, and a corresponding reverence for, life.

Secularism also spells a loss of mystery, a decline of the sense of transcendence. Life that is only horizontal crowds out miracle. An overemphasis on visibility blots out vision.

Leroy E. Loemker, writing on "The Nature of Secularism" says that "mediocrity is the first fruitage of the secular spirit.[2] When truth and morals become relative, when the human character is caricatured, when art becomes trivial, when tolerance means indifference, what is there left but an impoverishment in which glamor is a poor substitute for glory?

We find secularism expressing itself in economics and the related field of politics. Man easily becomes his own optician by fitting himself out with dollar signs as glasses. He may make a pretense of serving God, but the temple of Mammon, made with hands, is not far away. Not quite unwittingly he allows the Trojan horse of materialism to enter his home and influence his decisions. Politically he thinks of good times either in terms of rugged individualism or Leviathan.

In the last decades there has been a quiet revolution in our universities indicating a growing interest in the study of religion. This is a welcome sign because secularism had invaded education and had become a supporting atmosphere in colleges and universities adrift from the moorings of the churches. The American Academy of Religion and its Journal are supporting evidence. The phenomenon is encouraging, though it is the part of wisdom to withhold predictions. It seems that psychology and sociology still tend to replace theology and Christian philosophy. We are reminded of Paul Ramsey's 151st Psalm which begins like this:

> Oh! come, let us sing unto Sociology; let us
> heartily rejoice in the strength of our
> group consciousness.[3]

The rest of the song is a jolly exposure of the new idiom that seems to give some people status and stature.

The vexing problem of whether religion and Bible may or may not be taught in our public schools has brought confusion both in thinking and in practice. Fear of sectarianism has resulted in a neutralism in which secularism easily finds rootage. It may be safe to leave the teaching of religion and the Bible to the home and to the church, but according to some it may not be sound.

It is understandable that there are Christians who prefer a full-orbed training for their children, an education in which religion and the Word play a formative role. In a democratic society this is permissible and rewarding in the battle against secularism.

The fate of the smaller, church-related colleges in our country is hanging in the balance. Several factors are involved, but an important one is that the churches appear to have lost their zeal for a God-centered education. There is, of course, the perennial problem of the balance between academic freedom and the churches' concern where that concern is still evident. The solution does not lie in the bowing out of the field of education. When the Christian faith loses a comprehensive Christian view of life and the world, the absence of light and salt in the schools impoverishes the program.

The cost and upkeep of these smaller colleges is staggering. Grants from various sources are helpful. But the churches must be alerted to the significance of these bulwarks against secularism.

A study of contemporary literature gives content to T. S. Eliot's strong statement "that the whole of modern literature is corrupted by what I call secularism."[4] It is dull too; it cannot grasp the primacy of the supernatural which should be man's greatest concern.

The study of literature is very important because it reveals to us the pulse beat of modernity. Man has received a tremendous shock from the two wars of this century and their aftermath. Idealism and optimism have given way to realism, naturalism, and pessimism.

Hemingway tells us that there is no remedy for anything in life. Steinbeck reminds us that what God formerly took care of man must now take upon himself. A character in Sherwood's "The Petrified Forest" says that he belongs in the world of petrified stumps and fragments where even death has little or no meaning. In "Nightmare with Angels" Stephen Vincent Benét, asserting the bankruptcy of a machine civilization admits that we will not be saved by General Motors, or cheap housing, or Marxian dialectic, or church conferences, or vitamins, or the expanding universe.

John Killinger analyzes the writings of our times and sees in them the lostness of man because he has lost God. The pale Christ-figures are quite ineffectual. They do not stand up nor stand out. They represent the ideals of humanism, a secularization of Christ with no resurrection and no triumph.

There was a time, as in Dante's day, when man was surrounded by the presence of God. There was a time when men searched for the Holy Grail. Today man is in quest of himself on a rather fruitless search. Our writers know a great deal about evil, but in terms of the phenomenal rather than the noumenal. What was once the cosmic struggle has become a skirmish between the Id and the Ego. Such varied authors as Faulkner, Farrel, Hemingway, Steinbeck, Porter, Bellows, and others unconsciously give us the picture of man in his misery as the Heidelberg Catechism expresses it in its first part. Something of grandeur may occasionally shine through, but redemption is an atmosphere foreign to them.

Alienation and gloom compose the theme of the existentialists such as Sartre, Kafka, Camus, and their disciples. The self faces the meaningless, the tragic, the absurd with only enough courage left to face death with a minimum of quiver.

Secularism in the Churches

Contemporary criticism of the Church proceeds from two different points of view. There is the charge that secularism has invaded many churches to an alarming degree. With that criticism we are concerned in this section.

There is the other charge that the churches have been too other-worldly and have shied away from a healthy secularization, from an essential Christian worldliness. With this emphasis we shall deal more fully in Chapter XIII.

Since God has become a blur to millions, the churches are also affected. Where a congregation becomes the gateway to the country club, where lectures and harmless homilies ten miles from any exposition of a text beguile the listeners, where sin and atonement are toned down, where love loses the content of faith and doctrine, where Jesus is sentimentalized and demythologized, where inactive members remain just that, where people can no longer understand biblical terminology and prefer a new idiom, there secularism has also made its inroads. (The idolatry of idiom can also become "a tale told by an ['idiom,'] full of sound and fury, signifying nothing.")

We are well aware of the charges made by Bishop Robinson in his *Honest To God* and by Harvey Cox in *The Secular City*. The writings of Dietrich Bonnhoeffer are brought in to bolster the charges, although there are other emphases in this Christian martyr's convictions that should not go unheeded.

Though we need not and cannot agree with all the reasoning and all the conclusions of these critics, we do well to heed any warnings. Institutionalized Christianity is no substitute for a personalized faith and love. A God only far away is not the Christian's God. Christendom can be such a far cry from Christianity, as Kierkegaard said emphatically long ago. Clericalism may crush the spirit. The noise of our solemn assemblies easily drowns out the voice of Jesus Christ.

Churches concerned only with themselves are quite ineffectual in the world. Religion concerned too much with itself is "spiritual incest," as Samuel Miller says.

The fault does not lie with God. His not being there for many follows from man's not being there.

> I turned to speak to God
> About the world's despair;
> But to make bad matters worse
> I found God was not there.
>
> God turned to speak to me;
> (Don't anybody laugh)
> God found I was not there,
> At least not more than half.

The Remedy

If the churched and the unchurched feel comfortable in the presence of religion, they may not feel quite so comfortable in the presence of theology. For some folk, theology is unintelligible; for others it is unnecessary. But for the churches it is essential because it is their concern to grasp the self-disclosure of God. In the light of the divine revelation life has meaning, purpose, and destiny.

From the Biblical center shines God's revelation by which we come to understand man's tragic plight and the only escape from it. God in Christ as the center of the center alerts us to the triviality of our petty loyalties.

There are those who desire a new terminology to clarify God's relation to us. But is God as "the ground of our being" more meaningful than God as Father and Jesus Christ as Shepherd? The later designations have nothing to do with a three-story universe in which God might get lost.

Christ is very much with us as the Redeemer and the Transformer of man. He is also the Transformer of the secular, of the best in culture. H. Richard Niebuhr in his book, *Christ and Culture,* maintains that Augustine and Calvin taught this emphatically.

As Christians we must beware of our docetic tendencies. In our concern for personal salvation we tend to overlook Christ's significance for the whole divine plan. We fail to understand the relation of the supernatural to the natural. The former is not a distortion of the latter but its fulfillment. In his *Philosophy of Revelation* Bavinck quotes J. Christian Blumhardt as saying that man needs a twofold conversion, first from the natural to the spiritual life and then from the spiritual to the natural.

Scripture itself gives us the image of wholeness that we as Christians do not always seem to appreciate. The Hebrew writers speak of the God who may hide Himself from our comprehension but who also leaves a great deal for our apprehension. The heavens declare His glory; the little hills skip before Him; the pastures are fat because of His goodness. His voice rides on the winds. His law is meant to be hidden in men's hearts.

Jesus hallowed the natural, even taking the form of man. His resurrection assures ours. The Book of Revelation speaks of a new heaven and a new earth, the re-creation to which we look longingly. The Word teaches us the significance of creation. The secular world is a province to be reclaimed for the Kingdom of God.

"Holy worldliness" is not as radical a teaching as some of our contemporaries seem to think. It was not invented within the last few years anymore than breathing was. Unfamiliarity with the Word of God in all its reaches and with a theological position that honors the Absolute Sovereignty of God may cause people to respond to what they consider a new emphasis. The emphasis has been here for a long time, ever since the Almighty has spoken. It is up to man to hear and to do.

Purity of doctrine should always be matched by purity and sincerity in our lives. We are called to be the men and women of Christ, suffering in the life of the world. It will not do to flee the secular, but to be God's agents in sanctifying that realm.

Gerald Kennedy reminds us that we must spiritualize the material and materialize the spiritual. Only a true sense of stewardship and of our high calling will bring that about. The Christian is called, not only *from,* but also *for* a task. Man has both privilege and responsibility. In the light of revelation the Christian should understand that.

The follower of Christ should have his feet on the ground but his head in God's sunlight. His pilgrimage should be marked, not so much by speed, as by high seriousness within the atmosphere of divine revelation. It is Paul Scherer who reminds us that the world has not been changed so much by those who have both feet on the ground as by those who have one foot in heaven.

The rising tide of secularism will never inundate the City of God. This calls, not for a ghetto existence, but for a strong faith that has both content and the power to revolutionize where man's revolt has failed.

With deep humility and only in the strength of Christ Christians may chant:

> For we are the movers and shakers
> Of the world forever, it seems.

NOTES

1. Samuel Miller, *The Dilemma of Modern Belief* (New York: Harper and Row, 1963), p. 8.
2. Leroy E. Loemker, *The Christian Faith and Secularism* (New York: Abingdon-Cokesbury, 1948), p. 16.
3. Paul Ramsey, *Nine Modern Moralists*: *Christian and Otherwise* (Englewood Cliffs, New Jersey: Prentice-Hall, 1962), p. 26.
4. T. S. Eliot, *Essays Ancient and Modern* (New York: Harcourt, Brace, 1936), p. 110.

XII

The Church in a Changing World

The human spirit is alarmed and at times depressed because of the political, economic, social, and moral ferment in the world. A ferment of considerable proportions is evident also in the Church and the churches. Time was when the Church and the Christian faith were attacked from outside. Today the blows come from within the Church. Clergymen and theologians are waging a civil war that has aroused even a torpid world.

Such bloodless attacks can be more arousing than alarming. In the land of the dead there are no civil wars. A Church alive enough to criticize itself and to withstand criticism is not in danger of being written off. The lively debate issues in the cry for renewal, a rethinking of the nature and function of the Church, and a reassessment of the Christian faith in essence and in action.

Some of the questions from outside and from within are extreme. They seem to be motivated by the spirit of a questioning world. The traffic of interrogations is, however, not a one-way affair. The Church need not be afraid of questions; but it also has the right and the duty to ask them. This requires a spiritual equipment that will guarantee the right, the best answers and questions.

Do we know what the Church of Jesus Christ is and what it ought to be? Do we know the revelation of God in the Scriptures without which there would be no Christian faith and no Church? Do we know the history of God's people throughout the centuries well enough to differentiate between the essential and the peripheral? Are we a vital part of it, or are we bystanders watching a parade and perhaps hurling taunts or stones?

Critics of the Church, who are not always in agreement among themselves, have been saying that the Church has been too self-perpetuating, with too little concern for taking the faith out into the streets where it should make an impact. It suffers from smugness and snugness.

The charge is also made that the Church is too divisive. Such fragmentation is a far cry from a unified proclamation in word and deed.

There is also an other-worldly emphasis which blinds Christians to the social, economic, and political problems that plague the world. The attitude of "Heaven is my destination" spells indifference to the social implications of the Gospel. It is a question of the relevance or irrelevance of much that is proclaimed.

The criticism is also offered from within the churches that the institutional church is far too clerical. The cleavage between the clergy and the lay people is too great. What is the basis for, the nature of, the office of the ministry? Where does ordination begin and where does it end? These are significant questions especially in the face of the proliferating ministries in the churches. And in the last analysis is not every Christian a minister, a witness both in word and in deed?[1]

Because of the fermentation, a process never hurried, pat answers may be futile. Perhaps the best way to answer lies in the careful consideration of what the Church is, what its functions are, and what the telling renewal would imply.

It is better that the Church should ask these questions and provide answers than that the world should do this. A professional in his field is more of an authority than a non-professional. The Church based on the Word has been around for a long time, and its thoughts are long, long thoughts.

What Is the Church?

In the Old Testament the people of God, especially the assembly met for worship, are known as the called. The New Testament word *ecclesia,* church, is used by our Lord in Matthew 16:18 and 18:17. There are those who deny the authenticity of these verses, maintaining that the early church read this usage into Jesus' sayings. The traditional view, which honors the prophetic insight of the Son of God, accepts the Matthean record. Many passages in the New Testament speak of the church as an assembly of worshipers, as a closely knit group of believers, as the body of Christ of which the Lord and Saviour is the Head. That body is also a *koinonia,* a fellowship, a community, a communion.

On Pentecost Day that Christian fellowship came alive with the outpouring of the Holy Spirit. This was the power and illumination which Jesus had promised. Henceforth the proclamation of the Gospel spread from Jerusalem around the Mediterranean Sea and throughout the world. In the impressive expansion of Christianity churches were founded far and wide. The story of these churches is the history of the Church of Jesus Christ.[2]

The older dogmatics makes several distinctions in regard to the character of the Church. Today such distinctions may receive a frown or a smile, but mention of them may help to clarify.

There is the Church militant engaged in a warfare for the good and against evil. Those who are opposed to the use of military terms in the spiritual and moral realms should recall that the Word itself speaks of the full panoply of the Christian warrior and of fighting the good fight. It tells of spiritual powers of darkness assailing the cause of Christ.

There is also the Church triumphant whose members have crossed to the other side beyond the reach of evil and death. No longer under the cross, theirs is the victory and the crown.

Mention is also made of the Church visible and invisible. It is visible in the faithful lives of its members and in the ministry of the Word and sacraments within those places of worship we call churches. It is invisible in this sense, that we cannot say with precision who the genuine members are. These, however, are known to God. This should take care of the quip once made that no one can love an invisible bride.

The Church is both organism and organization or institution. As an organism it is the body of Christ made up of many members, each dependent on the others and primarily on the Head. Its organization is evident in its offices, government, and activities.

There are descriptive attributes of the Church which can be understood only in the light of the Word. These are unity, holiness, and catholicity.

Unity implies the mystical union of believers with Christ and therefore with one another. The faithful are branches of the Vine, members of the Body. They are stones in the spiritual building arranged in the proper grouping with Christ as the chief corner stone.

Holiness indicates that the faithful are saints in Christ. Paul addresses the churches as those who are called to be saints. The New Testament knows nothing about canonization of a select few who have attained sainthood. All the redeemed who have been declared just and who are taking their sanctification seriously are saints, not perfect, but striving by divine grace.

The Apostles' Creed speaks of a holy, catholic church. Catholicity means universality. All believers of all ages, in every land make up this Church. The spiritual unity, the holiness are there in this universal body whose members believe in the Father, the Son, and the Holy Spirit.

That the Church could reveal more unity, holiness, and catholicity is a perennial charge. But this is not something that was discovered in the twentieth century. Those sincere members of the churches who know their calling as well as their imperfections are aware of it. They know better than the uncommitted that sanctification is a slow but steady process. This in no way denies that the full commitment of every Christian is more of an ideal than a reality. It is here that criticism from within and without should bear fruit.

The Functions of the Church

The Church has its privileges and also its duties. Its functions are clearly stated in the Word of God. That these have not been carried out perfectly is no denial of the divine mandate nor of the ideal that beckons.

The first task of the Church is the true and lively preaching of the Word. Our Lord gave His people the Great Commission to preach the Gospel and to baptize in the name of the triune God. The proclamation has eternal and temporal, spiritual and moral implications. The Word is not to be diluted. Harmless little homilies or lectures on current events and opinions are poor substitutes. Much is made today of the relevance of the Gospel to our predicament. But relevance means the application of something. That all-important something is the unadulterated Gospel which alone can heal the sickness of our civilization. When the man in the pulpit reads a passage from Scripture and walks miles away from the text, what is the relevance? Or when the man in the pulpit worries a text from a doctrinal perspective without touching on our problems that keep shouting, what is affected?

"Thus saith the Lord" applies to all the ages of man. "This is my beloved Son; hear ye him" still demands listeners and response. Without the divine revelation man is lost on the moors of history and in the mists of self-deception.

Another task of the Church is the proper administration of the sacraments. It is evident from the Gospels and the Epistles that Christian baptism and the Lord's Supper must never be separated from the Word. These sacraments are for believers and their children and are not to be peddled out of sheer sentimentality. They imply both privilege and responsibility and a growing awareness of the meaning of sainthood. Damage done by custom and superstition can be repaired only by a return to the living Word.[3]

Baptism and the Lord's Supper are dramatic actions proclaiming divine grace. The two tests for their particularity are that they are significantly related to the historic Christ, and they reveal the central message of redemption. Our vital response in faith and gratitude makes us the participants we ought to be.

A third function of the Church is discipline. In many areas of the Church less has been made of it than of the other two. Calvin, who writes clearly on the three functions, stresses discipline as a bridle, a spur, and a rod.[4] The power of the keys of which Jesus speaks in Matthew 16:19 and the binding and loosing mentioned in Matthew 18:18 are entrusted to the churches. It is the minister and the ruling elders who receive members into the church on confession of faith and the promise to be loyal and true.

The vow made before the elders and in the presence of the congregation implies sincerity, faithfulness, and loyalty. Christian care, counseling, admonition, and in some instances more severe measures are essential to the purity and health of the churches. Severity must be tempered with gentleness in the spirit of Christ. Wherever discipline is relaxed, the body of Christ becomes weaker. Churches have paid dearly for neglecting this function. In I Corinthians Paul warns what must be done with an offending member.

It is interesting to note that Dietrich Bonhoeffer, to whom appeal is often made by the radical critics of the Church, emphasizes the essential exercise of discipline for the sake of holiness. He considers it "a servant of the precious grace of God."[5] As such it is not only the task of ruling elders but also of all members of the churches concerned about the brotherhood.

The Church has a mission in and to the world. For long years it has done that through missionary enterprise and in the area of Christian education. What should not be forgotten is the unpublished witnessing of many outside of the walls of church buildings. It should be remembered today when the cry for renewal is echoed by the sounding of alarm bells.

Criticism of the Church has stirred up a ferment especially in the area of its mission in society. Winds from different directions have caused more than a stirring in the mulberry trees. The popular mind that was not touched by the teachings of Karl Barth, Emil Brunner, Reinhold Niebuhr, and Paul Tillich has caught a bit of fire from the more popular and startling works of Bishop Robinson, Harvey Cox, and Pierre Berton.

Such writings, with or without benefit or understanding of Tillich and Bonhoeffer, stress Christian worldliness and religionless Christianity. The churches are accused of bottling up faith and of indulging in self-perpetuation. Faith must be taken out of the churches and practiced in the streets. The emphasis is more on activity than on the faith.

Robinson's writings, not too carefully thought out in regard to content and practical application, have scuttled much of the Word and a Christian theology based on it. What is left for anyone to take into the streets is not anything particularly Christian. The furore aroused by *Honest To God* has not stirred people to greater action. It is reported that on Easter Day 3 per cent of the population of London attended the churches. It is not reported that the other 97 per cent were exercising a faith that moves mountains or even society.

Harvey Cox in *The Secular City* proposes that secularization is the liberation of man from religious and metaphysical tutelage. He distinguishes between secularization and secularism which easily becomes another orthodoxy. He presents Jesus as coming to us through social change rather than ecclesiastical tradition. Urbanized-secular man, living in technopolis, is really not interested in what he considers an outmoded world-view.

Cox, though appealing to Scripture, is more of a sociologist than Biblical theologian. His thesis is arousing but not devastating. One gets the impression that technopolis should dictate to the Christian faith. There is no suggestion that Jesus is weeping over secularized technopolis.

Berton's *The Comfortable Pew* should be read, not only by those who attend church regularly, but also by those who are responsible for the empty pew, who prefer the more comfortable bed or the open spaces to the assembly of worshipers. Homeless prodigals are hardly the best critics of home and the Father.

Critics of the Church easily bypass the three functions of the Church. That gives them a wide field to play in, but the game is not entirely fair. Nor is any church true to its calling if it minimizes these functions. The full preaching of the Word touches on all of life. The proper understanding of the sacraments contributes to holy living in the world. Respect for discipline does more for a maturing faith and practice than sentimentality which is not love.

Radical criticism is also subject to criticism. Raising the roof and neglecting the foundation is foolish procedure. A watering down of the Word and of the Christian faith will never Christianize the world. The Church of Jesus Christ, aware of its blemishes, confessing its faults, proclaiming the Gospel that is to be believed and lived, is still here and will remain. If it had put a premium on faith at the expense of works, it would have perished long ago. If it had emphasised works and scuttled the faith, it would have been more shortlived still.

The Ecumenical Movement

Much is being written today about renewal, togetherness, and merger. Some denominations have united and more are in the planning stage. Appeal is made to Jesus' prayer: "That they may all be one," and to Paul's question: "Is Christ divided?"

The presence of denominations and sects has been called the scandal of Christianity. It is not all scandal, however, unless one is ready to call the Reformation and the Wesleyan Revival scandalous interruptions. There are historical reasons for the many-branched tree of the Church.

Division can also be looked upon as distribution. The physical universe has a rich diversity. An orchestra also has. In these there is a togetherness in diversity. If from one point of view the situation in the churches looks chaotic, from another point of view one can still discern "one Lord, one faith, one baptism." The universality expressed in the Apostles' Creed is not a mirage.

Doctrinal differences have caused divisions, but national, ethnic, and cultural factors are also present. As political differences do not necessarily destroy a nation, so varied emphases have not destroyed the Church. There is a classic statement that the Church is there where the Word is rightly preached and the sacraments are properly administered. That is basic though not static. Christians must go on from there, putting faith into practice in every area.

It is the sectarian spirit that damages the unity of the Church. Harm is caused by the confusing of essentials and non-essentials. Purity of Biblical doctrine should be a major concern, but purity of life, easily stained by moral heresies, should be equally so. Faith without works of love is sterile.

It is here that dialogue in the spirit of humility is essential. Striving for greater unity requires understanding. The dialogue among Protestants and between Protestants and Roman Catholics is a stirring that should be welcomed. Hopes which tend to skyrocket should be guided and tempered by the faith which gives content and direction. A united front of the churches is not solidified if Scripture is watered down and the basic confession is glossed over. A united body in which all distinctions and distinctiveness are erased would be more of a fool's paradise than the Church.

All talk and action in regard to mergers should make a careful distinction between the Church as organism and as institution. Ecclesiastical machinery is inescapable, but the

Church needs a prophetic ministry far more than the organization man. Secularism in pulpit and pew will not Christianize the world. A genuine, distinctive Christian faith, thriving on divine revelation, must be taken into the streets where the lions are. But lions and lambs will never lie down in togetherness unless the Lamb is proclaimed in word and deed.

A word should be said about the National and World Councils of Churches.[6] They have drawn warm support and also severe criticism. In the discussion heat is unavoidable, but light is essential.

These Councils are not churches, nor do they aim at one super-Church. They were formed because the need was felt for conversation, cooperation, and a united Christian witness to a world in upheaval. The Church must witness in a time of social and technical revolutions and against ideologies that defy the Lord of life.

The Councils have been criticized for pronouncements considered outside the primary task of the Church, and for more emphasis on action than on the basic faith. When such criticism comes from within the membership, so much the better. It is dialogue that makes for clarification.

It should be remembered that the National Council limits membership to communions confessing "Jesus Christ as Divine Lord and Saviour," and that the World Council confines membership to such communions as confess "the Lord Jesus Christ as God and Saviour according to the Scriptures."

It should be recalled that the World Council of Churches is the outgrowth of historic conferences on Missions, Faith and Order, Life and Work, and that at meetings of the Council there has been strong debate between the theological conservatives and impatient activists. The Evanston meeting is a case in point.

For those really concerned it would be enlightening to read the writings of two ecumenical leaders. Visser 't Hooft's *No Other Name* is a strong defense of the Christian faith over against a challenging syncretism. Hendrik Kraemer's

Why Christianity? pulls no punches in asserting the unique-
ness of the Christian religion over against those who blithely
and ignorantly maintain that one religion is as good as another. Such strong defences can be offensive only to those
who confuse the shaking of the foundations with their destruction.

Is refusal to join the Councils or withdrawal from them
the most effective way to proclaim the Christian faith and
all its applications? Or is the certain sound of the trumpet
within the assemblies a better way? The healing of differences
is not accomplished by suspicions, prejudices, aspersions, but
by a courageous faith motivated by God's love for us and
our love for Him and His directive Word.

The heroes and heroines of faith are not in a private gallery but in the Church, in the assemblies, and in a confused
world where man has lost his way. They are more than
echoes of the Voice that says, "Hearken unto me."

NOTES

1. See two rewarding pamphlets: *For the World,* a study book
   prepared for the 1966 General Assembly of the National
   Council of Churches; and *Christian Response to the Technical
   and Social Revolutions of our Time* (United Presbyterian
   Church in the U.S.A., January-February, 1966).
2. Philip Schaff and K. S. Latourette tell the story well.
3. See Karl Barth, *The Teaching of the Church Regarding
   Baptism* (London: SCM Press, 1954).
4. John Calvin, *Institutes of the Christian Religion,* trans. Henry
   Beveridge (2 vols.; Edinburgh: T & T Clark, 1895), IV,
   chap. 12.
5. Dietrich Bonhoeffer, *The Cost of Discipleship* (New York:
   Macmillan, 1960), pp. 324 ff.
6. See Paul Carson, *God's Church — Not Ours* (Cincinnati:
   Foreward Movement Publications, 1965).

XIII

Morals Old and New

By indirection the revolution in morals and the radical approach to ethics drive home again the age-old conviction that morality cannot be separated from religion and, for the Christian, from revealed religion. Inverting Emerson's words we might say: When the gods go, the half-gods arrive. A man-decided ethics is the fruit of man's self-assertion over against the God of revelation. There is a definite connection between the God-is-Dead theology and the scrapping of the old morality. If God is no longer absolute, the revelation of His will in Law and Commandments must also give way to a relativistic factor in all ethical judgments.

Situation Ethics

Men like Bishop John A. T. Robinson, Canon Rhymes, and Joseph Fletcher are among the leading exponents of the new morality. If we are shocked by their radical teachings, we can also be goaded to serious thinking. Christian faith is not only a matter of "the ramparts we watch." It implies taking the offensive under orders from the Captain whose revelation we may not deny. We who stand for the old morality and its application to new situations may at times agree with those who take the relativistic approach. An intelligent understanding of that approach, however, will reveal how widely apart the evangelical and the radical are from the very starting point.

The exponents of situation ethics scrap all absolutes except the absolute of love which must consider the welfare of all concerned.[1] The inductive, empirical approach, which is dangerous, is far better than the deductive. Persons are more important than principles. Moral worth is an achievement by the individual. Norms are to be worked out by experience. Values are not real, but nominal. Good and evil are extrinsic, contingent, contextual. No action is good or right in itself. The important matter is whether an action benefits or hurts people.

According to Robinson God's Word is there, not as proposition but as presence.[2] There is no such thing as *a* Christian ethics. Honesty is essential for finding a basis for moral action. "Built-in moral values" should guide us. We need working rules, but these must be based on love, not on law. There should be no judging of others, no legalistic interference. This requires a steady maturing in which the spirit overcomes the flesh.

Fletcher stresses love and reason as most important. Only love is constant.[3] God gives himself to everyone, both believers and unbelievers. The divine love has nothing to do with commands. Even monotheism, the belief in one God, cannot be commanded. We must love God in our neighbor, for he does not ask us to love him exclusively. Love and justice are the same. Love justifies the means.[4]

This author, like others, emphasizes the functional, the pragmatic, the useful. Like Bentham and Mill he is concerned about the greatest good of the greatest number. Good and evil are not properties, but predicates or attributes. Conscience is a function, not a faculty. It works in a given situation with no absolutes but love.

The appeal of these writers rests in large part on their presenting special situations. They insist that even those who stand for the old morality practice situation ethics in such matters as war, race, and capital punishment. There is no full-scale agreement in these instances. Why then can there not be personal, moral decisions in cases where no absolute rule applies?

Take, for example, the matter of sex and sex taboo which, by the way, makes the new morality a luscious plum. These men admit that sex without love is wrong, and also that some rules are necessary but not as absolute law in every situation. Pre-marital sex relations may be good provided there is love, deep concern for the other. Prudery does more harm than good. Fletcher maintains that a harlot can do good by breaking the Seventh Commandment. He tells the story of a sailor disturbed by his loss of virility, and torn by fears of lost identity. A harlot restores his self-respect and gives him psychic freedom from his sex fixation.

He also tells the story of a woman captured by the Russians and separated from her family for years. The only way she can be sent home is to become pregnant. In this situation she chooses to do this and as a result is sent home. She is reunited with her family and together with the child that is born they seem to live happily ever after.

There are other situations with which we are perhaps more familiar. May a physician or surgeon resort to the ethical lie when all hope of recovery is gone? Must we tell the truth when an enemy knocks at our door to take away an innocent person? Have we thought of the bombing crew that rained destruction on Hiroshima? It is reported that the captain of the bomber cried out, "My God, what have we done?"

We must admit that these instances and many more like them are not a matter of easy solutions by reference to a little book of rules. Reasoning in love is far more difficult than rationalization on the basis of an easy ethics. The old ethics has been concerned about it for centuries and at its best has offered no pat solutions. The Word of God is also very much concerned about it though it gives no little lists for each special occasion. What it does do, however, is **lay** down some basic absolutes which the new morality refuses to recognize.

Critical Evaluation

If the conservatives are criticized for having an easy ethics, the radicals propose an easier one. Loving your neighbor or loving God in your neighbor may sound like a very simple solution to those who have denied God and scuttled most of His revelation.

Where have the ethical empiricists learned about this love? What must one think of their selectivity when they ignore the Biblical relationship between love and the Christian faith? The Word says that God is love; it nowhere states that love is God. Fletcher blithely insists that love is the Holy Spirit. If this is not near-blasphemy, it is very bad theology. Man rewriting revelation can propose just about anything.

God is not only loving; He is also holy. He does more than suggest holiness; He commands it: "Be ye holy; for I am holy." Jesus summarizes the law, telling us to love God above all, and our neighbor as ourselves. When He commands us to love one another, He bases it on the right relationship to God. That is always the logic of Scripture. Jesus came to fulfill the Law, not to abolish it. His Cross speaks loudly of grace and of judgment, of love and that divine wrath which cannot tolerate evil and sin. It is true that our Lord criticized the legalism of the Pharisees severely as Paul opposed the legalism of the Judaizers. These charges against a righteousness by works can be leveled also against the radical moralists who insist on the practice of love at the expense of unmerited grace.

When love is emphasized outside the framework of salvation, sin gets less than a passing nod. To ignore man's tragic plight from which he cannot extricate himself is to make salvation meaningless.

The attempt to separate ethics from the full teaching of

Jesus and the Word, taking what one pleases from Scripture and scrapping the rest, is neither scholarly nor ethical. To say, for example, that our age of anxiety is an age of honesty is a bit of casuistry slanted in favor of the unrepentant rebel and against the honest Puritan.

The radical moralists have a rather naive conception of human nature. They exemplify a romanticist attitude stressing man's mastery in a given situation. How does one become mature in Christian love? Talking about it without telling how it can be acquired is nebulous. How does one become a responsible person? Can that be done without prohibitions? What does love in the right situation mean to a young couple unchaperoned in a hot-rod, or to the stripper in Soho who tauntingly climbed on the roof of Billy Graham's car? Moral maturity implies spiritual maturity. Selfish rationalization is not high knowledge. It certainly is no substitute for wisdom. Moral certitude requires a greater framework than immediate experience. As Tom Driver writes: "Freedom from law is an achievement, not a birthright."[5]

If the exponents of the new morality are tired of absolutes and authority, they are tiring in their bowing to science, technology, pragmatism, and Freud. Instead of dialogue with the God of revelation they prefer monologue. They simply substitute one authority for another, man's mastery for the Master. Their modernity is as old as man's first rebellion.

Their insistence that values are ephemeral outdoes the ancient pagans who thought better of them. Their dogma that conscience is only a function, that only usefulness counts is a benighted casuistry, a bit of emoting rather than clear thinking. Their substituting of a contemporary prejudice for the tyranny of tradition has the earmarks of a new sophistry.

It is true that Robinson speaks of a need for the transcendent in our moral decisions. But what is that which is transcendent? Is it Kant's moral imperative, or Emerson's Over-Soul, or Carlyle's Everlasting Yea, or the God of revelation about whom we must be very honest?

It is a bit surprising how choosy the new moralists are. They still need Jesus, though they scrap most of His cardinal teachings about God and man. There is nothing new about their silence concerning Jesus Christ as Lord and Saviour. When morality is loosened from its genuine Christian moorings, one needs only the Moral Teacher steps ahead of Buddha. But even those steps need serious explanation.

In their emphasis on being practical in the ethical situation the radical advocates are less than helpful. They decry sex taboos and magnify love as concern for the other person or persons. But who is to guarantee that love remains unadulterated when passion takes over and rationalizes its activities? Is love present in pre-marital relationships, or is there a higher kind of love that forbids and restrains, calculating all consequences, listening to the Voice that precludes monologue? And how can there be love in extramarital relationships which imply broken vows, broken hearts and homes, and the living of a lie?

Was the sailor who gained his psychic freedom from a sex fixation by benefit of a harlot really freed and healed? Or is this only another instance of the sex obsession of our day, the revolt against chastity lampooned as prudery? In such an a-moral climate it seems a bit trite to insist that sex without love is wrong when freedom and license are not clearly defined.

The new moralists strongly advise that the Church must take the lead, become the herald in denouncing the old morality and proclaiming the new. But those who are in the pews may have a deeper conception of love than that which the new "gospel" offers. And the majority who are not in the pews can hardly be considered authorities on what Jesus means by love. Will these honor the Church's proclamation more by loving God and His revelation less? Is man's mastery of love in a given situation merely a human accomplishment or does it require a wisdom from above revealed in that

Word entrusted to the Church, that Word which cannot be ignored with impunity?

The More Excellent Way

Instead of the Church's knuckling down to a naturalism and humanism which are as new as the oldest heresy, it has the mandate to proclaim the whole Word of God in all its religious and moral implications. When Saint Paul wrote the Corinthian church of a more excellent way, he poured out his soul in that most exquisite hymn on love. But I Corinthians 13 cannot be lifted out of its context. The apostle's central message resounds with a glorying in Jesus Christ crucified. That is the divine love which alone can inspire and educate our love for God and man.

The Church's task is to proclaim the full Word of God, not a fraction of it to suit man's infantilism or dotage, or his latest sophistication. That Word stresses atonement and the moral life, and in that order. Man in his rebellious state needs restoration to that blissful seat from which he has fallen. Man cannot rise to higher levels on stepping stones of his dead self.

A Christian ethics demands a closer scrutiny of faith, hope, and love in their relatedness.

Christian faith is not ambiguous. There is nothing vague about its trust, confidence in, knowledge of, and commitment to a personal God in whose will is our peace. God's will, revealed in His Word, in Jesus Christ, and illumined by the Holy Spirit, is our absolute. He alone can make saints out of sinners, justify us by faith in Him. That faith, as Bonnhoeffer says, is also obedience.

Christian hope is not a plucking of the last unbroken string on a harp, but the assurance that our hope is anchored within the veil where Christ, the Pioneer, has gone before us.

Christian love is the response of the redeemed life to God who is love. It is the expression of gratitude for so great a salvation. Our love to God must bear fruit in our love to our fellowmen. The logic of salvation is clear.

Something should also be said about law and grace. Here again Scripture clarifies where rebellious man so easily confuses. The Old Testament gives us the Law and the prophets for which Jesus had such great respect. It was not law as the will of God but legalsim against which our Lord protested. It was not the will of God but the works righteousness of the Judaizers against which Paul contended. Because man could not and cannot save himself by fulfilling the Law, Jesus came to fulfill it. That is how the believer escapes the curse of the Law and the divine wrath against sin. Justified by faith he must now live increasingly under the law of love, the royal law, the perfect law of liberty as James speaks of it. This requires the wisdom that is from above, which is pure, peaceable, gentle, full of mercy and good fruits (James 3:17). Paul in Galatians and Romans lays tremendous stress on the right understanding of law and grace. We are not to sin that grace may abound; on the contrary we are to live the sanctified life because the old life has died, has been buried, and has risen with Christ.

The absolutes of the divine revelation of grace can save us from petty moralisms but also from rebellious rationalization. The Word militates against lists of ultra-puritanic rules and also against anti-puritanic license. It emphasizes serving God through loving Him and our neighbors. Such serving implies gift, privilege, task, and responsibility.

How must we regard the Ten Commandments in our day? Are they still absolute, or obsolete? The Scriptures must shape our judgment. In the light of grace the Commandments still have significance for us. They are a revelation of God's being, of His mighty acts of freeing His people for a greater accomplishment, and of His will. That Law reminds us of our inadequacies and of our plight without divine grace. It cannot redeem us, but it points us to Christ who came to fulfill all righteousness. Our Lord gives us the abundant life motivated by our love for God and our fellowmen. Salvation is an escape, not from the divine will, but from petty legalisms and rebel fallacies.[6]

Much has been written about conscience which plays a large part in the moral life. The radical moralists prefer to speak of it as a function rather than a faculty. The Old Testament stresses the heart as motivating man's decisions. Whereas the Greeks thought of conscience especially as causing pain because of wrong actions, the New Testament views it from a positive and negative point of view. The thirty-one occurrences of the word make a fascinating study. Conscience can be good or weak and defiled. It can accuse or excuse. More than a function it relates motivation and action to the higher authority of God.

Conscience has been called the voice of God, the bond between law and responsibility, the bond between duty and obligation, and the super-ego of Freud who really dethrones conscience. Waddams refers to it as "the personality passing judgment on what is right and wrong."[7] Lillie speaks of it as the natural reaction of the Christian's entire being developed under Christian influences.[8] Lehmann insists that only from and within the Christian *koinonia,* the fellowship, can conscience acquire "ethical reality and the power to shape behaviour through obedient freedom."[9]

The New Testament is far more concerned about the sanctity than the dignity of the individual. Applying that concern to situation ethics, especially in regard to the sex obsession of our time, we hold that love in the right situation can never be separated from holiness and purity. Loving God in Christ, believing obediently are a far more excellent way than canonizing Faust, Don Juan, or Peer Gynt. Taking a cue from Kierkegaard's *Either-or,* we maintain that sexual democracy leads only to boredom and frustration. Man needs the religious and ethical stages to come to fulfillment.

NOTES

1. For their ideas see articles in *Religion and Life* (Nashville: Abingdon Press, Spring, 1966).
2. John A. T. Robinson, *Christian Morals Today* (Philadelphia: Westminster Press, 1964).
3. Joseph Fletcher, *Situation Ethics: The New Morality* (Philadelphia: Westminster Press, 1966).
4. *Ibid.*, p. 95.
5. Tom Driver in *Religion and Life* (Nashville: Abingdon Press, Spring, 1966).
6. For a good presentation, see Elton Trueblood's *Foundations for Reconstruction* (New York: Harper, 1946).
7. Herbert Waddams, *A New Introduction to Moral Theology* (New York: Seabury Press, 1965), p. 83.
8. William Lillie, *Studies in New Testament Ethics* (Philadelphia: Westminster Press, 1963), p. 56.
9. Paul Lehmann, *Ethics in a Christian Context* (New York: Harper and Row, 1963), p. 366.

XIV

Destiny and Destination

It requires more than a computer to analyze and summarize the fascinating subject with which we have been dealing in these chapters, the relation of the Christian faith to culture. There are those who like John Cowper Powys and John Erskine have dealt with the complete life and the meaning of culture.[1] Others have written more positively from the Christian perspective. If truth, goodness, and beauty are there for the seeking and the finding, will these cease to be when the last human life is ended, when history will have run its course, and the universe lies shriveled and dead? Or will there be endless time and endless living, generation after generation becoming only a memory? Or is there a greater hope, a firmer assurance that destiny and destination are not the product of human dreams but of a compelling faith?

Immortality

There have been and there are those who have not been inspired by such a faith or by any hope. Lucretius has his modern offspring. Someone has blatantly written:

> Don't bother me now; don't bother me never;
> I want to be dead forever and ever.

Scepticism is evident from words carved on a tomb: "I was not, I became; I am not, and I care not." Swinburne in "The Garden of Proserpine" tells us "that dead men rise up never, and even the weariest river winds somewhere safe to sea." Bertrand Russell sees only gloom and doom for man. Albert Camus states frankly, "I do not like to believe that death opens upon another life. To me it is a door that shuts."

To these mild or wild despairers we address the pointed question:

> If after all that we have lived and thought
> All comes to Nought —
> If there be nothing after Now,
> And we be nothing anyhow,
> And we know that — why live?

John Baillie expresses surprise at the indifference of those who do not desire life after death.[2] If they do not prefer it for themselves, would they say at the deathbed of one dearly loved: "I don't care"? If the desire is there for those we esteem, why not for ourselves?

Reflections on immortality have nurtured several theories. The biological and social theories have stressed the immortality of the race or of influence.[3] But there is pale comfort in the thought that the human race may cease, and the universe itself come to an end as scientists have maintained.

The impersonal theory of pantheism, disloyal to personality, also offers small consolation. Hinduism, Buddhism, Stoicism, and Absolute Idealism speak of a melting into the great All, a scrapping of individual personality, the asset we cherish so much in this life. Even Buddha refused to answer when asked if Nirvana meant a state of being or total extinction.

The hope of immortality has, however, been more than a spark in the human heart. Plato wrote touchingly of that hope. Socrates looked forward to release from the prison of his body. The Hindu writes of laying aside his worn-out robes and taking new ones. The American Indian dreams of the Happy Hunting Grounds.

It is the Christian conviction that man is living in what

Teilhard de Chardin has called the Divine Milieu. It is in that environment that eschatology takes on significance. Change and decay are inevitable. Death is incontrovertible. What lies beyond the human scene, beyond the farthest bounds of time and space? The answer lies in that faith which lays hold of the Living God and trusts with ardent expectancy in the divine fulfillment.

The Christian, accepting that divine revelation which rounds out the meaning of life, looks beyond death and the complicated framework of this world to what is laid away for those, who living in the City of Man, have persistently dwelt in the City of God. For him death and the final stoppage of time are not *finis* but new beginnings.

Resurrection

The Christian conviction, based on God's revelation in His Word, is far more compelling and re-assuring than the speculations of unaided reason. Immortality is a pale doctrine compared with that of the resurrection.[4]

There may be a logic of hope in the pyramids and the country churchyard, but the Christian hope is more firmly established.

Though the Old Testament speaks sparingly of the life after death, what amazes us is the Hebrews' strong faith in the Living God and joy in His presence. Such assurance precludes the gloomy thought of extinction. In Psalm 16:10-11 we read: "For thou dost not give me up to Sheol, or let thy godly one see the Pit. Thou dost show me the path of life; in thy presence there is fullness of joy, in thy right hand are pleasures for evermore." Psalm 17:15 speaks of beholding God's face in righteousness on awaking. Psalm 49:15 refers to the soul's ransom from Sheol and being received by God. Psalm 73:23, 24 resounds with the conviction of the divine presence, guidance, and welcoming to glory. Psalm 139 sings of the inescapable Presence and pleads for being led in the way everlasting.

Enoch's translation, Elijah's fiery chariot, and Job's faith in his Redeemer or Ransomer may cause the sceptic's shrug but also assures the believer that Israel's faith looked beyond this life.

In the little apocalypse of Isaiah (chaps. 24-27) there is a definite hint as to the resurrection. In Isaiah 26:19 we read: "Thy dead shall live, their bodies shall rise. O dwellers in the dust, awake and sing for joy. . . ." Daniel 12:2, 3 speaks of the awakening of those who sleep in the dust.

In the intertestamentary period belief in the resurrection became more pronounced. The Pharisees in Jesus' day held to it. Martha at the grave of her brother confesses that he will rise again in the resurrection at the last day. It was on this occasion that our Lord uttered those profound words: ". . . I am the resurrection and the life; he who believes in me, though he die, yet shall he live" (John 11:25).

The whole of the Word reveals a personal God, not an abstraction, the fruit of speculation. Throughout it also honors personality and a personal relationship between God and man. It is evident from the lives of the Old and New Testament saints and from Jesus who warned against harming His little ones and ministered to persons as no one else has ever done so lovingly. It is reasonable to conclude that a personal God does not desire the extinction of those He created in His image. He wishes believers to share His eternity, for He cares for them.

The Incarnation of our Lord hallowed the body and matter. By virtue of His suffering, death, and resurrection He guaranteed our resurrection, an immortality not grasped by pagans ancient or contemporary. On and after that first Easter those early Christians proclaimed their Living Lord and were assured that after life's fitful fever they would rest in the Lord and after time's restless course had ended they would rise from the dead on the last day.

Paul in I Corinthians 15 proclaims the resurrection against doubters and for those who accept the full revelation in

Jesus Christ. He even ties that assurance to the full impact it should make on daily living. For if God is everlasting, and death has been conquered, life expressed as love for God and our fellowmen is worth living indeed.

The Book of Revelation rounds out the revelation and gives us a perspective beyond time, history, and tragedy. It is poor reasoning to excuse it as apocalyptic and therefore as less reliable. The descriptive language of poetry has always been essential to religion. The Bible abounds in it for the simple reason that the soul's invincible quest demands more than logic which easily comes to the end of its tether.

The last book of the Bible tells glowingly of that "divine event to which the whole creation moves." As Genesis reveals beginnings, so this book describes the ending of the old and the dawn of the new.

The new has already taken hold in the lives of those who believe in God and are born anew. Jesus tells us that he who believes in the Son has eternal life. And Paul reminds us that if we are risen with Christ, we must seek the things that are above. This eternal life is not subject to the temporal, where successiveness is our lot. It has nothing to do with quantity but everything to do with quality. It has significance for time, but its fulfillment must await the final end of time. Here also, not speculation, but revelation enlightens us.

The Consummation

Scripture relates the general resurrection and the fulfillment of eternal life to the return of Jesus Christ. His Second Coming in judgment to usher in the new heavens and the new earth is an article of faith held by most evangelicals. There are those who are puzzled by the descriptive language of apocalyptic and yet recognize the givens of eschatology, that time and history must end, that good will triumph over evil, and that the new age of peace and righteousness will finally come.[5] There are others who fuss and fume over dates and particulars, forgetting that poetry arrives at truth beyond literal confines.

The Christian sanely guided by Scripture believes that Jesus will return as He has promised. This conviction inspired the early Christians though they were wrong as to the time of His coming. It has inspired the Church for two thousand years and will go on doing so. The specific thrust of the New Testament is that Christians must preach the Gospel and live it, leaving the consummation to God whose wisdom is unfailing.

In our century much has been written about realized eschatology. C. H. Dodd, who has modified his position somewhat, is representative of this school of thought.[6] Emphasis is laid on Jesus' continual coming throughout the centuries with little regard for His final coming. Though it excludes too much of what Scripture teaches, it tends to check too great a preoccupation with our Lord's return. Such preoccupation is apt to minimize the divine plan for the ages and man's calling in time and history.

What the Word teaches believers is that they must always live in expectation, not idly but laboring while it is day. Parables dealing with vineyards, stewardship, and talents bring this home clearly. We should recall that the last prayer in the Word is: "Come, Lord Jesus." That prayer must be expressed in the midst of our busy calling. In other words Jesus is constantly knocking at the doors of our lives, our families, our homes, society, and every rich area of life. And the urgency is stimulated by the assurance that He will come again at the end of time.[7]

His coming will be in judgment. It is true that we are living under judgment each day and that man throughout the ages has never escaped it. But final judgment is also inevitable. Good must triumph over evil, right over wrong, peace over conflict. The day will come when Jesus Christ, despised, rejected, crucified, will return victorious; and every eye shall see Him, even those who pierced Him with haughty unbelief.

The terrifying thought of judgment does not appeal to many minds and hearts. Christian scholars of the stamp of Karl Barth and John Baillie stress the love of God and the triumphant, redemptive work of Christ to the extent that they wonder how God can condemn anyone forever. These men do not deny the divine wrath and judgment nor the urgency of repentance, but for them the all-encompassing love of God must ultimately be victorious.[8]

This hinting at universal restoration, already found in Origen, also brings its problems. If there is to be a measure of punishment for unbelief, where and when will that take place? Would it not necessitate a kind of Purgatory? If the entire human race is bound to be saved, what difference will it make whom or what one believes or how one has lived? And what becomes of the urgency of the Gospel?

The Bible nowhere speaks of a universalism. On the contrary it stresses the wrath of God against all sin and unrighteousness and never separates that wrath from the divine love. Jesus gave solemn warning about the great separation at the end time, and the rest of the New Testament emphasizes that judgment from which there is no recall. The proclamation of the Gospel is evidence that God's grace, the well-meant offer of salvation, is not to be trifled with. Acceptance or rejection brings its reward.

We must beware of confusing our vindictiveness with the righteousness of God. Bavinck warns us against hasty judgment either in a positive or negative sense in regard to the salvation of those noble pagans who sought the good life and those who die in infancy without benefit of believing parents. He adds that the Reformed confession, stressing the boundless mercy of God and the free offer of grace, is neither narrow nor cribbed.[9] It leaves judgment in the hands of God, not of man. It is the Christian's concern, not to populate hell, but to proclaim the Good News, the accepting of which guarantees citizenship in the Kingdom of everlasting peace.

After resurrection and judgment the life everlasting will experience its full adventurous content in the new heavens and the new earth. By divine grace the regeneration of man will find its completion in the regeneration of creation. The poetic description of the New Jerusalem in Revelation is a this-worldly picturing of other-worldly realities. All that is true, noble, righteous, pure, lovely, and worthy of praise are brought together in the City of God, the renewed creation revealed in its highest glory and richest beauty. This final consummation fulfills, rather than annuls, the essential meaning of man in the universe under God. Biblical apocalyptic, marked by the high seriousness of great poetry, is prophetic expression of the Christian faith and hope that the divine plan and purpose will be fully realized.

Problems remain which will not be solved until faith becomes clearer sight. If civilization and culture have their end as *finis,* will there not be a significant residual in the life to come? Are there not prospects for a renewed culture to which our categories of time and space are but faint approximations? When personality, God's great gift to man in time, is perfected, not destroyed, and the image of God is fully restored, is it not likely that progressive activity will be the lot of the blessed? In Revelation 21:24-26 we read that the glory and honor of the nations shall be brought into the New Jerusalem. Such is the inheritance of grace for the redeemed who walk there. Not boredom, but the great adventure awaits them.

The impact of revelation as to man's destiny and destination should arouse him to serious living. Propelled by the future, he becomes more than a stranger and a pilgrim here, experiencing the tension, the tuggings of nature and of grace. By divine mercy the wholeness of the Christian view of life and the world assures him that he is numbered with the saints who seek and find a City. Looking forward to that final transfiguration which is his inheritance, he relishes, with Adelaide Procter, "joys tender and true, yet all with wings — so that earth's bliss may be [his] guide and not [his] chain."

Man, the thinking reed, needs the reenforcement of a faith that is given, and a love that will not let him go. It is only by divine revelation that he can come into the inheritance of the children of God who in Christ have learned that love is the greatest of these, greater than faith and hope, more comprehensive than truth, goodness, and beauty.

NOTES

1. John Cowper Powys, *The Meaning of Culture* (New York: Garden City, 1941).
   John Erskine, *The Complete Life* (New York: Julian Messner, Inc., 1943).
2. John Baillie, *And the Life Everlasting* (New York: Scribners, 1933).
3. George Eliot's "The Choir Invisible" is an example.
4. Oscar Cullmann, *Immortality of the Soul,* or *Resurrection of the Body* (New York: Macmillan, 1958).
5. See Reinhold Niebuhr, *The Nature and Destiny of Man* (New York: Charles Scribner's Sons, 1943).
6. See for example, C. H. Dodd, *The Parables of the Kingdom* (New York: Scribners, rev. ed., 1961).
7. T. F. Torrance, *When Christ Comes And Comes Again* (London: Hodder and Stoughton, 1957).
8. See Gerrit C. Berkouwer's criticism in *The Triumph of Grace in the Theology of Karl Barth* (Grand Rapids: Eerdmans, 1956).
9. Herman Bavinck, *Gereformeerde Dogmatiek* (Kampen: J. H. Kok) IV, pp. 810, 811.